A-Z LINCOLN

CONTENTS

Key to Map Pages	2-3
Map Pages	4-37
Large Scale City Centre	38

Index to
Villages,
& selected ... of interest

REFERENCE

A Road	A57
B Road	B1188
Dual Carriageway	
One-way Street Traffic flow on A roads is also indicated by a heavy line on the driver's left.	
Road Under Construction Opening dates are correct at the time of publication.	
Proposed Road	
Restricted Access	
Pedestrianized Road	
Track / Footpath	
Residential Walkway	
Railway	Level Crossing / Station
Built-up Area	
Local Authority Boundary	— · — · —
Posttown Boundary	
Postcode Boundary (within Posttown)	— — — —
Map Continuation	12 / Large Scale City Centre 38

Car Park (Selected)	P
Church or Chapel	†
Cycleway (Selected)	
Fire Station	■
Hospital	H
House Numbers (A & B Roads only)	2 75
Information Centre	i
National Grid Reference	490
Police Station	▲
Post Office	★
Speed Camera with Speed Limit Fixed cameras and long term road works cameras. Symbols do not indicate camera direction.	30
Toilet: without facilities for the Disabled with facilities for the Disabled	▽ ▽
Educational Establishment	▭
Hospital or Healthcare Building	▭
Industrial Building	▭
Leisure or Recreational Facility	▭
Place of Interest	▭
Public Building	▭
Shopping Centre or Market	▭
Other Selected Buildings	▭

SCALE

Map Pages 4-37   1:19,000

0	¼	½ Mile
0	250	500	750 Metres

3.33 inches (8.47cm) to 1 mile   5.26cm to 1km

Map Page 38   1:9,500

0	⅛	¼ Mile
0	100	200	300 Metres

6.67 inches (16.94cm) to 1 mile   10.53 cm to 1km

Copyright of Geographers' A-Z Map Company Limited

Fairfield Road, Borough Green, Sevenoaks, Kent TN15 8PP
Telephone: 01732 781000 (Enquiries & Trade Sales)
            01732 783422 (Retail Sales)

www.az.co.uk
Copyright © Geographers' A-Z Map Co. Ltd.
Edition 5 2012

 Ordnance Survey® This product includes mapping data licensed from Ordnance Survey® with the permission of the Controller of Her Majesty's Stationery Office.

© Crown Copyright 2012. All rights reserved. Licence number 100017302
Safety camera information supplied by www.PocketGPSWorld.com
Speed Camera Location Database Copyright 2012 © PocketGPSWorld.com

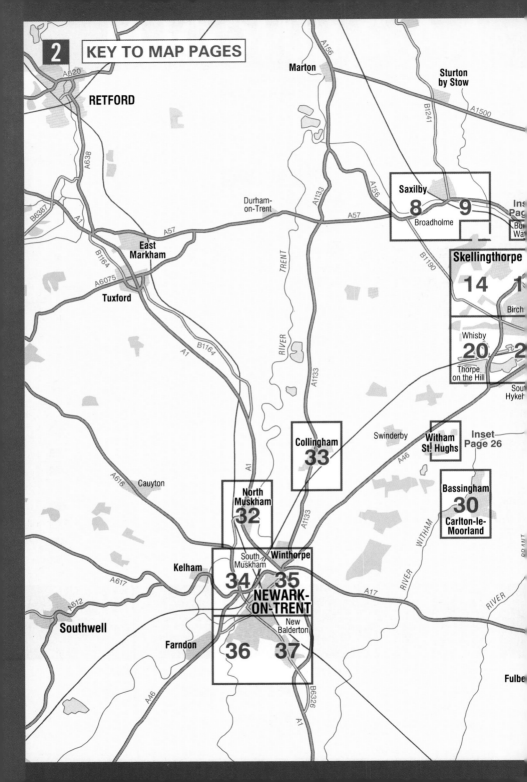

2 KEY TO MAP PAGES

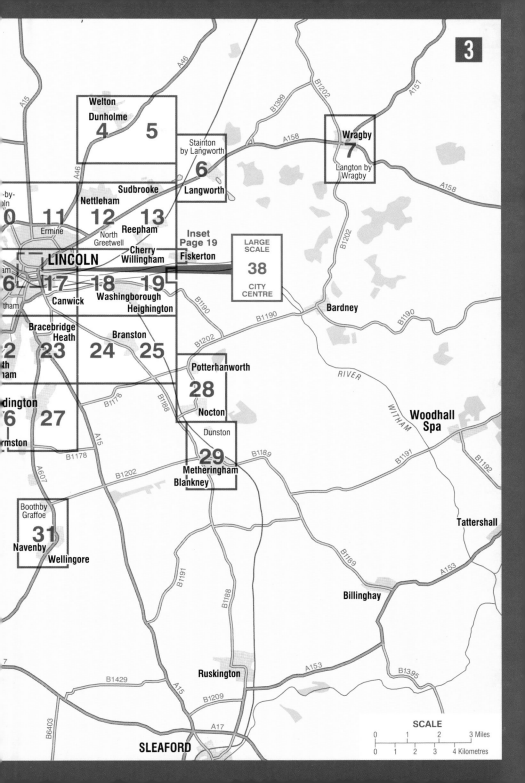

3

Welton
Dunholme
4 **5**

Stainton
by Langworth
6
Langworth

Wragby
7
Langton by
Wragby

Sudbrooke
Nettleham
12 **13**
Reepham
North
Greetwell

0 **11**
Ermine

Inset
Page 19

LARGE
SCALE
38
CITY
CENTRE

LINCOLN
Cherry
Willingham
Fiskerton

6 **17** **18** **19**
Canwick Washingborough
Heighington

Bardney

Bracebridge
Heath
2 **23** **24** **25**
Branston

Potterhanworth
28
Nocton

RIVER

WITHAM

Woodhall
Spa

dington
6 **27**
rmston

Dunston
29
Metheringham
Blankney

Tattershall

Boothby
Graffoe
31
Navenby
Wellingore

Billinghay

Ruskington

SLEAFORD

SCALE
0   1   2   3 Miles
0 1 2 3 4 Kilometres

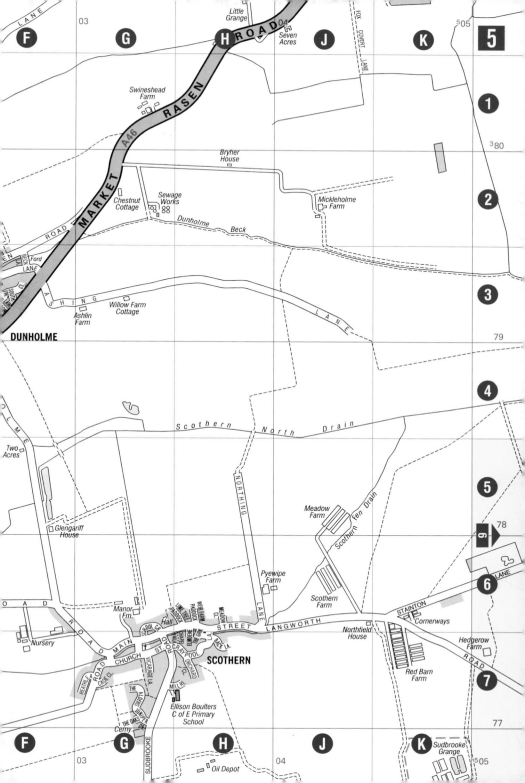

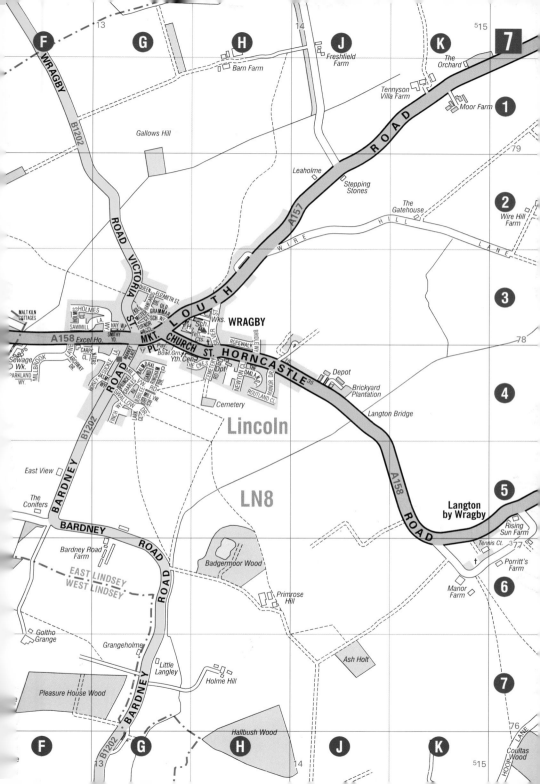

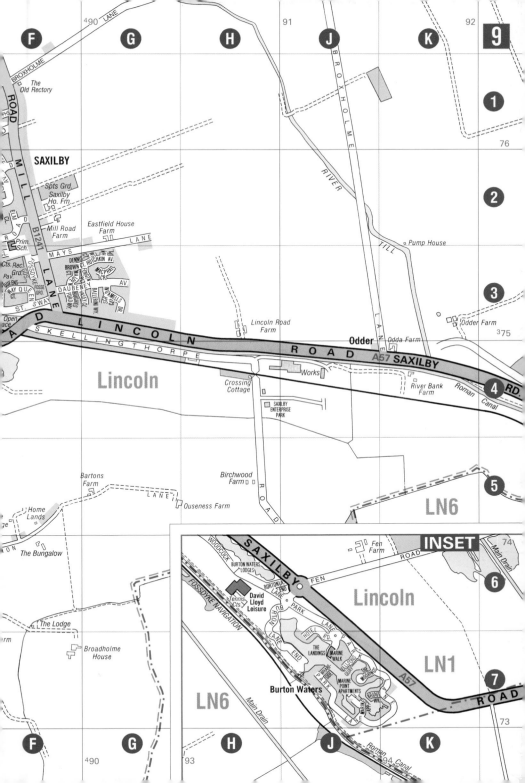

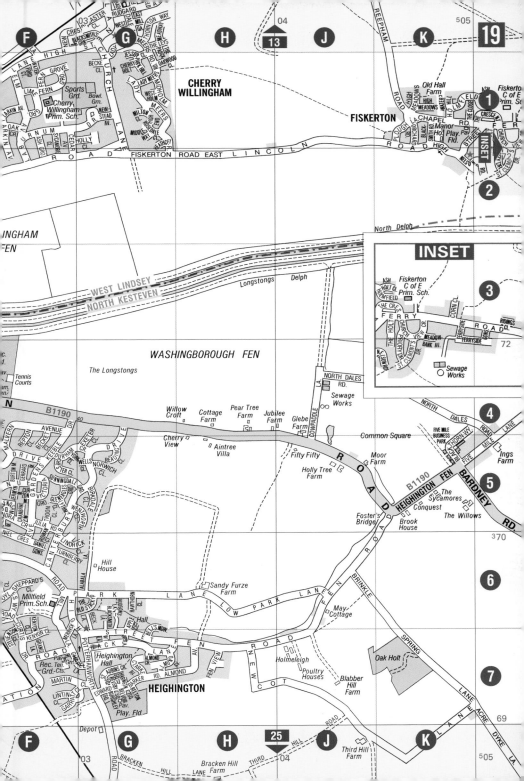

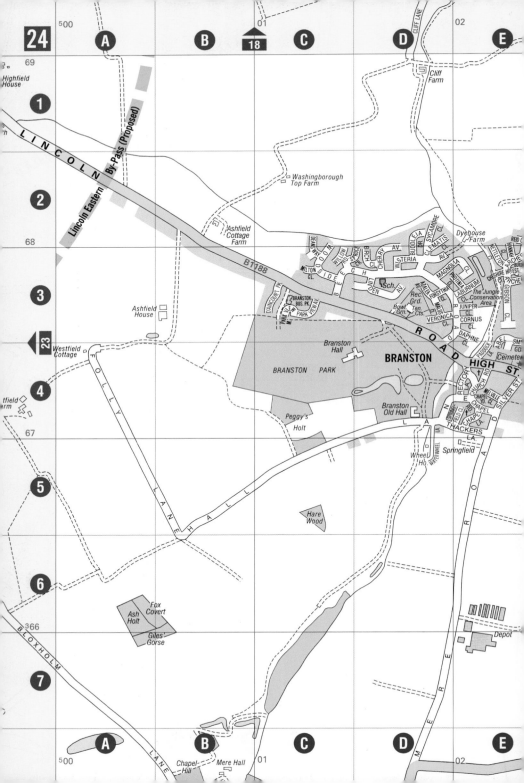

500

69

A B C D E

01 02

18

Highfield
House

1

LINCOLN

2

Lincoln Eastern By-Pass (Proposed)

68

Washingborough
Top Farm

Ashfield
Cottage
Farm

B1188

3

Ashfield
House

BRANSTON BUS. PK.
PARK VW.
DAUNCOURT PK.
PARK VW.
VISTA

DEANSWAY
WILLOW
BIRCH
CHERRY
AV.
WISTERIA
LINDEN
MILTON
CL.
WOODSIDE
BENTLEY
AZALEA
AV.
Sch.
RYLAND

BUDDLEIA
CLEMATIS CL.
SYCAMORE CL.
MAGNOLIA
CHESTNUT
FORSYTHIA
LABURNUM CL.
JUNIPER
VERONICA
CORNUS CL.
CL.
DAPHNE CL.
PAXINIA

Dyehouse
Farm

REID CL.
NETTLETON
HANNAH CR.
ARCHER
GIBSON
CHESHIRE
FOREST

The Jungle
Conservation
Area

Rec.
Grd.
Ten.
Cts.
Bowl
Grn.

Branston
Hall

BRANSTON

ROAD
HIGH ST.

SM.
GD.
Cemetery

23

Westfield
Cottage

HOLLY

4

field
rm

BRANSTON PARK

Peggy's
Holt

Branston
Old Hall

Chapel

RECTORY
CHURCH YD.
FIELD CL.
MELVILLE
CHAPEL LA.
SILVER ST.
THACKERS
LA.
LA.

Springfield

67

Wheel
Ho.
WATERWHEEL

LANE

HALL

5

Hare
Wood

6

Fox
Covert

Ash
Holt

Giles'
Gorse

Depot

366

BLOXHOLM

7

LANE

MEREE ROAD

500

A B C D E

01 02

Chapel
Hill

Mere Hall

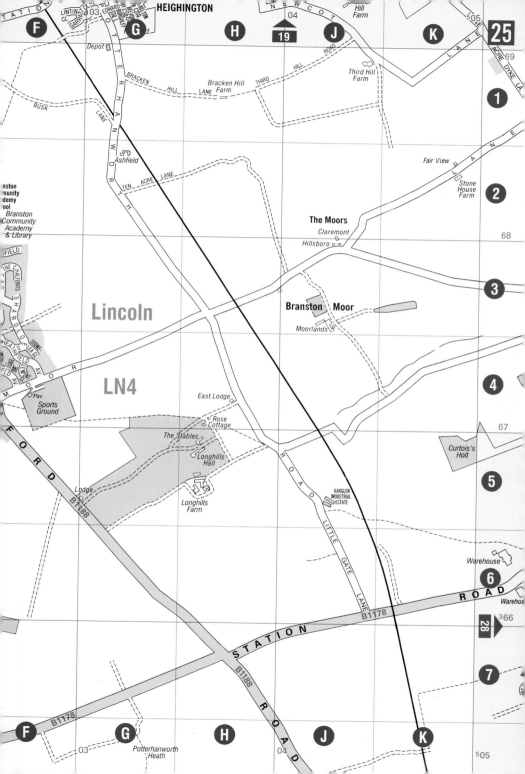

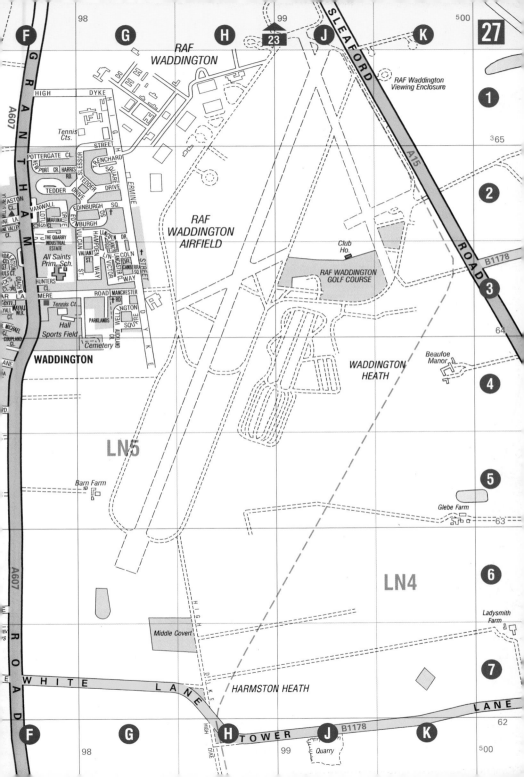

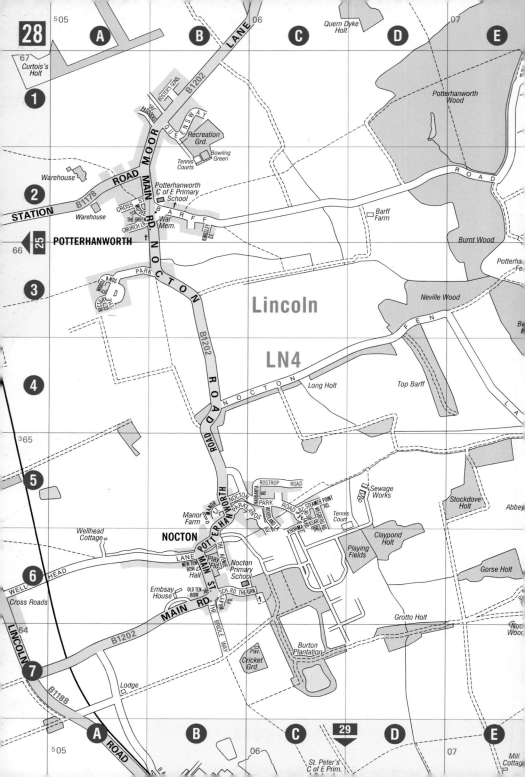

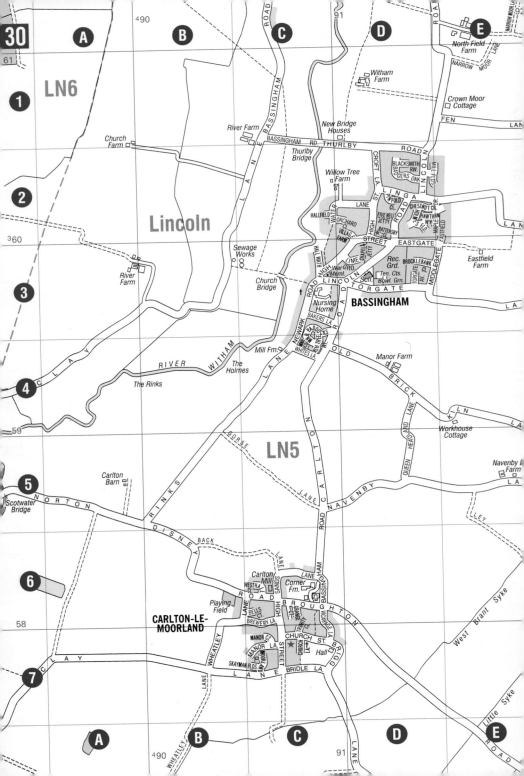

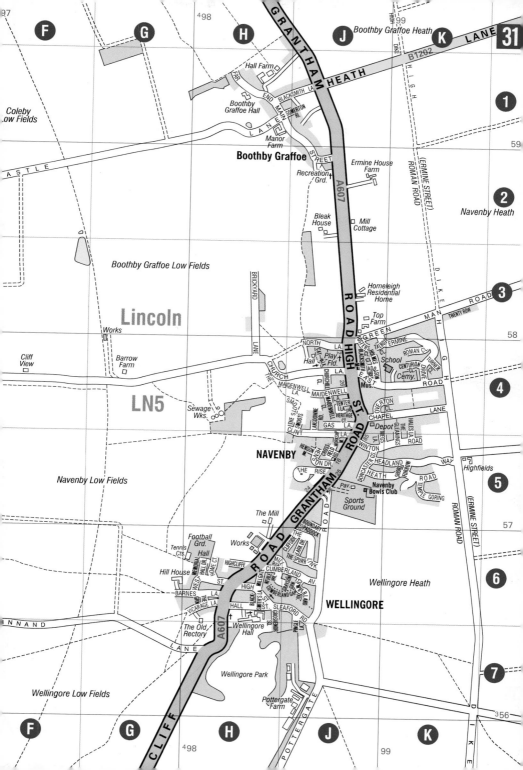

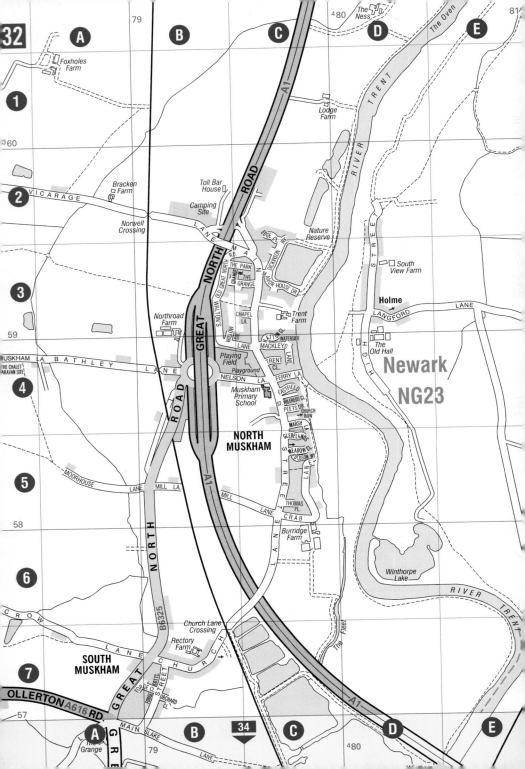

WINTHORPE

FOSS WAY (ROMAN ROAD)

Newark Golf Centre
(Driving Range)

Bowling Green

Service Area

Service Area

Winthorpe Crossing

Cricket Ground

Comm. Cen.

Winthorpe Prim. Sch.

Nursing Home

Elk Racing Outdoor Karting Circuit

Airfield (disused)

Newark Showground

Lingspot Farm

Newark & Notts Gliding Club

Newark Air Mus.

Airfield (disused)

Depot

Depot

Depot

Brunel Dr. Workshops

Enterprise Park

Depot

Works

Depot

Factory

Works

Playing Field

Depot

Works

Depot

Newark Bus. Pk.

Brunel Bus. Pk.

Works

Beaconfield Farm

NG24

Cotswold

Coddington

Black's Farm

Coddington C of E Prim. Sch.

Moat

Beacon Hill Conservation Park

Reservoir (covered)

Nursing Home

Recreation Ground

Windmill

LINCOLN

AVENUE

Prim. Sch.

Comm. Cen.

Newbridge Works

BEACON

HILL

BECKINGHAM

NEWARK ROAD

A1

A46

A17

A1133

A1

B6166

This page is a map of New Balderton, Balderton, and Fernwood.

Key labels visible on the map:

Grid references (top): F, G, H, 35, J, K, **37**

Grid references (right side): 1, 2, 3, 4, 5, 6, 7

Grid references (bottom): F, G, H, J, K

Grid coordinate numbers: 83, 53, 52, 51, 50, 81, 82, 83

Major place names and features:

- Nursing Home
- Recreation Ground
- Barnby Rd. Academy
- CROMWELL RD
- CLAY LANE
- Barnby Crossing
- GROVE COTTAGES
- BARNBY ROAD
- Football Ground
- Highfields School
- Green Hill Farm
- Football Ground
- The Grove Leisure Cen.
- The Grove School
- **New Balderton**
- Playing Field
- Cressy Holme Farm
- Field House Farm
- Bowl. Grn. Pav.
- Playing Field
- John Hunt Prim. Sch.
- Chuter Ede Prim. Sch.
- Fen Lane Farm
- Sports Ground
- Lowfield Works
- Sewage Works
- **BALDERTON**
- Jericho Works
- **Fernwood**
- Comm. Cen.
- Balderton Hall
- Fernwood Bus. Pk.
- GREAT NORTH RD
- HOLLOWDYKE
- HUNDRED ACRES LANE
- CROSS LANE
- STAPLE LANE
- GRANGE LANE
- B6326
- A1

Street names include: CHARLES STREET, VERNON ST, HILL ST, NEWTON ST, WRIGHT ST, HUE GDNS, TUDOR DR, THE AVENUE, NICHOLAS DR, ELM CL, FALSTONE AV, BANCROFT RD, MARTON RD, BEESTON RD, MILTON AV, LINDEN AV, GROVE STREET, GLEBE PARK, SHAKESPEARE ST, ORCHARD CL, COWAN, WILLOW, HAZEL, GREBE CL, KINGFISHER, FOXGLOVE, SMITH CL, HOLLY M, FAIRFIELD ROAD, BAINES AV, WARWICK RD, WARWICK CRES, WEST WARWICK CT, KNOTT'S CT, MACAULAY, TENNYSON, WORDSWORTH, KEATS RD, COLERIDGE RD, CHAUCER RD, SHERIDAN, BRISBANE, DRYDEN, ELIPSHAM RD, GOLDSMITH RD, BROOKE CL, COLBURN, BULLPIT ROAD, CODDINGTON ROAD, WOLFIT AV, CLEMENT AV, STEELES DR, SPRING, HOLLOWDYKE, SOUTHFIELD, QUEENS ROAD, CHURCH LANE, MAIN STREET, MANNERS ROAD, MARSTON, HADDON, APPLEBY, PRIORY DR, BANKS CL, HARBY, COTTAGE, LOVERS LANE, MEAD WAY, BELVOIR RD, MOUNT PL, STAFFORD RD, WILFRED AV, LANSBURY, RUSSELL AVENUE, CHRISTOPHER CR, CATKIN WAY, GOLDSTRAW, WILLIAM HALL WY, CAMPION, CORMACK LA, DALE LANE, CARNELL LA, THOMAS RD, OAKFIELD RD, GILBERT WY, PHOENIX LA, CRESCENT, DOVEDALE TER, APPLE LANE, PAGET WY

Labeled circled numbers on roads: 30, 30, 30, 35

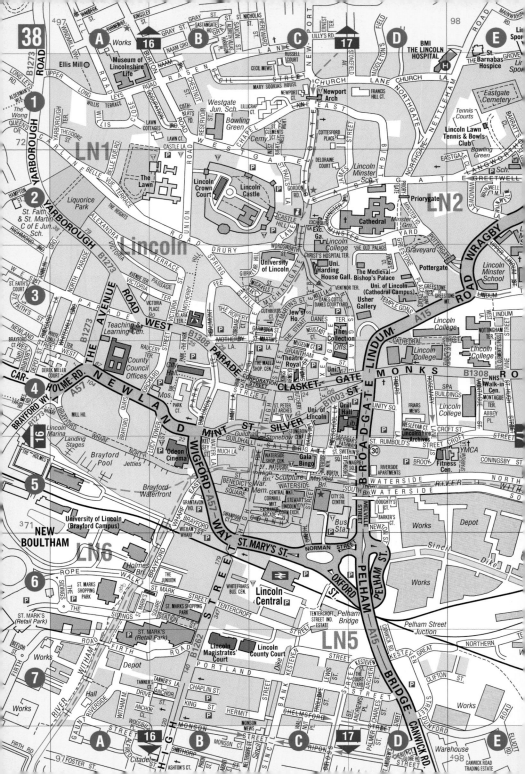

INDEX

Including Streets, Places & Areas, Hospitals etc., Industrial Estates,
Selected Flats & Walkways, Stations and Selected Places of Interest.

HOW TO USE THIS INDEX

1. Each street name is followed by its Postcode District, then by its Locality abbreviation(s) and then by its map reference;
   e.g. **Addison Dr.** LN2: Lin . . . .7H **11** is in the LN2 Postcode District and the Lincoln Locality and is to be found in square 7H on page **11**. The page number is shown in bold type.

2. A strict alphabetical order is followed in which Av., Rd., St., etc. (though abbreviated) are read in full and as part of the street name;
   e.g. **Beck Hill** appears after **Beckhead Pk.** but before **Beckingham Rd.**

3. Streets and a selection of flats and walkways that cannot be shown on the mapping, appear in the index with the thoroughfare to which they are connected shown in brackets; e.g. **Almond Wlk.** LN5: Well . . . .6H **31** (off Cumberland Av.)

4. Addresses that are in more than one part are referred to as not continuous.

5. Places and areas are shown in the index in BLUE TYPE and the map reference is to the actual map square in which the town centre or area is located and not to the place name shown on the map; e.g. **BALDERTON** 4H **37**

6. An example of a selected place of interest is Millgate Mus. 7C **34**

7. An example of a station is **Collingham Station (Rail)** 4J **33**

8. An example of a Hospital, Hospice or selected Healthcare facility is LINCOLN COUNTY HOSPITAL 2H **17**

9. Map references for entries that appear on large scale page **38** are shown first, with small scale map references shown in brackets;
   e.g. **Alexandra Ter.** LN1: Lin 2A **38** (2E **16**)

GENERAL ABBREVIATIONS

App. : Approach	**Flds.** : Fields	**Nth.** : North
Arc. : Arcade	**Gdn.** : Garden	**Pde.** : Parade
Av. : Avenue	**Gdns.** : Gardens	**Pk.** : Park
Blvd. : Boulevard	**Gth.** : Garth	**Pas.** : Passage
Bri. : Bridge	**Ga.** : Gate	**Pl.** : Place
Bldgs. : Buildings	**Gt.** : Great	**Ri.** : Rise
Bus. : Business	**Grn.** : Green	**Rd.** : Road
Cvn. : Caravan	**Gro.** : Grove	**Rdbt.** : Roundabout
Cen. : Centre	**Hgts.** : Heights	**Shop.** : Shopping
Circ. : Circle	**Ho.** : House	**Sth.** : South
Cl. : Close	**Ind.** : Industrial	**Sq.** : Square
Cnr. : Corner	**Info.** : Information	**St.** : Street
Cott. : Cottage	**La.** : Lane	**Ter.** : Terrace
Cotts. : Cottages	**Lit.** : Little	**Trad.** : Trading
Ct. : Court	**Lwr.** : Lower	**Up.** : Upper
Cres. : Crescent	**Mnr.** : Manor	**Vw.** : View
Cft. : Croft	**Mkt.** : Market	**Vs.** : Villas
Dr. : Drive	**Mdw.** : Meadow	**Vis.** : Visitors
E. : East	**Mdws.** : Meadows	**Wlk.** : Walk
Ent. : Enterprise	**M.** : Mews	**W.** : West
Est. : Estate	**Mt.** : Mount	**Yd.** : Yard
Fld. : Field	**Mus.** : Museum	

LOCALITY ABBREVIATIONS

Bald : **Balderton**	Farn : **Farndon**	Pott : **Potterhanworth**
Barl : **Barlings**	Fis : **Fiskerton**	Ree : **Reepham**
Barn W : **Barnby in the Willows**	Harby : **Harby**	Ris : **Riseholme**
Bass : **Bassingham**	Hard : **Hardwick**	Sax : **Saxilby**
Bath : **Bathley**	Harm : **Harmston**	Scot : **Scothern**
Best : **Besthorpe**	Hawt : **Hawton**	Skel : **Skellingthorpe**
Blank : **Blankney**	H'ton : **Heighington**	S Car : **South Carlton**
Booth G : **Boothby Graffoe**	Holm : **Holme**	S Hyk : **South Hykeham**
Brace H : **Bracebridge Heath**	Kel : **Kelham**	S Mus : **South Muskham**
Bran : **Branston**	Lang W : **Langton by Wragby**	Stain L : **Stainton by Langworth**
Bro : **Broadholme**	L'worth : **Langworth**	Swin : **Swinderby**
Brox : **Broxholme**	Lin : **Lincoln**	Thor : **Thorney**
Burt L : **Burton-by-Lincoln**	Lit C : **Little Carlton**	Thpe : **Thorpe**
Burt W : **Burton Waters**	Meth : **Metheringham**	T Hill : **Thorpe-on-the-Hill**
Can : **Canwick**	Nav : **Navenby**	Thurl : **Thurlby**
Carl M : **Carlton-le-Moorland**	Nett : **Nettleham**	Wad : **Waddington**
C Will : **Cherry Willingham**	N'wark T : **Newark-on-Trent**	Wash : **Washingborough**
Codd : **Coddington**	New B : **New Balderton**	Well : **Wellingore**
Coll : **Collingham**	New : **Newball**	Welt : **Welton**
Dodd : **Doddington**	Noct : **Nocton**	Whi : **Whisby**
D Noo : **Drisney Nook**	N Gre : **North Greetwell**	Wint : **Winthorpe**
Dunh : **Dunholme**	N Hyk : **North Hykeham**	With S : **Witham St Hughs**
Duns : **Dunston**	N Mus : **North Muskham**	Wrag : **Wragby**

A

Abbey Pl. LN2: Lin 4E **38** (3G **17**)	**Aberporth Dr.** LN6: Lin 6F **15**	**Acre Dyke La.** LN4: Bran 7K **19**
Abbey St. LN2: Lin 4D **38** (3G **17**)	**Abingdon Av.** LN6: Lin 1G **21**	**Adam Cl.** LN6: Lin 7H **15**
Abbotsford Way LN6: Lin 2C **22**	**Abingdon Cl.** LN6: Lin 1G **21**	**Addison Cl.** LN5: Nav 4J **31**
Abbot St. LN5: Lin 7B **38** (5E **16**)	**Acacia Av.** LN5: Wad 6D **22**	**Addison Dr.** LN2: Lin 7H **11**
Abbott's Way NG24: N'wark T 6F **35**	**Acacia Rd.** NG24: New B 3H **37**	**Adelaide Cl.** LN5: Wad 1D **26**
Abel Smith Gdns. LN4: Bran 4E **24**	**Acer Cl.** LN6: Lin 7H **15**	**Admiral Wlk.** LN2: Lin 1H **17**
	Acer Ct. LN6: Lin 7H **15**	**Adwalton Cl.** NG24: N'wark T 7J **35**
	Acorn Cl. LN5: Lin 7D **16**	**Affords Way** LN6: N Hyk 7F **21**
	NG24: New B 3G **37**	**Aima Ct.** LN2: Nett 1B **12**

Ainsdale Cl.—Beech Av.

Ainsdale Cl. NG24: Bald 6J **37**
Aisne Cl. LN1: Lin 6E **10**
Akeman Dr. LN4: Brace H 5G **23**
Akrotiri Sq. LN4: Noct 5C **28**
Alabala Cl. LN4: Wash 5E **18**
Alabala La. LN4: H'ton 6G **19**
Albany St. LN1: Lin 1E **16**
Albany Ter. LN5: Lin 2D **22**
Albert Av. NG24: Bald 4G **37**
Albert Cres. LN1: Lin 2D **16**
Albert St. NG24: N'wark T 1D **36**
Albert Ter. LN5: Lin 6D **16**
Albion Cl. LN1: Lin 7C **10**
Albion Cres. LN1: Lin 7C **10**
Albion St. NG24: N'wark T 7D **34**
Albion Works LN1: Lin 1D **16**
Alconbury Cl. LN6: Lin 1G **21**
Alder Cl. LN6: N Hyk 5K **21**
NG24: New B 3G **37**
Aldergrove Cl. LN6: Lin 7G **15**
Aldergrove Cres. LN6: Lin 7G **15**
Alderman's Wlk. LN1: Lin 1A **38** (2C **16**)
Alderney Way LN6: N Hyk 6A **22**
Alders, The LN2: Scot 7G **5**
Aldreth Vs. LN1: Lin 1B **38**
Alexander Av. NG24: N'wark T 3F **35**
Alexander Cl. LN4: Meth 5K **29**
Alexander Wlk. LN2: Lin 7K **11**
Alexandra Ter. LN1: Lin 2A **38** (2E **16**)
Alexandre Av. LN6: N Hyk 6K **21**
Alford Mill Cl. LN6: N Hyk 7H **21**
Alfred Av. LN4: Meth 5G **29**
Alfred St. LN5: Lin 7A **38** (5E **16**)
Allandale Cl. LN1: Lin 5D **10**
Allandale Vw. LN1: Lin 5D **10**
Allenby Bus. Village LN3: Lin 2K **17**
Allenby Cl. LN3: Lin 3K **17**
Allenby Rd. LN2: Lin 2K **17**
LN3: Lin 2K **17**
Alliance St. NG24: N'wark T 5E **34**
Allison Pl. LN1: Lin 2D **16**
Allison St. LN1: Lin 2D **16**
All Saints La. LN2: Nett 1B **12**
Allwood Rd. LN2: Dunh 3D **4**
Almond Av. LN4: H'ton 7G **19**
LN6: Lin 6A **16**
Almond Cl. LN1: Sax 2F **9**
Almond Ct. LN6: Lin 6A **16**
Almond Cres. LN4: H'ton 7G **19**
LN5: Wad 6D **22**
LN6: Lin 6A **16**
Almond Gro. LN6: Skel 2E **14**
Almond Ho. LN6: Lin 6A **16**
Almond Wlk. *LN5: Well 6H 31*
(off Cumberland Av.)
Alness Cl. LN6: Lin 6F **15**
"Alstom Power Millennium Sculpture, The" - Empowerment 5C 38 (3F 17)
Altham Ter. LN5: Lin 6E **16**
LN6: Lin 7D **16**
Althea Ter. LN3: Ree 4H **13**
Alumnia Ct. LN6: Lin 7A **16**
Alvey Rd. NG24: Bald 4J **37**
Alvis Cl. LN4: Brace H 5F **23**
Amble Cl. LN1: Lin 5E **10**
Ambleside Pk. LN6: N Hyk 6K **21**
Ancaster Av. LN2: Lin 1H **17**
Ancaster Cl. LN3: C Will 7G **13**
Ancholme Cl. LN1: Lin 5D **10**
Anchor Cl. LN5: Lin 7A **38** (4E **16**)
Anchor St. LN5: Lin 7B **38** (4E **16**)
Anderby Cl. LN6: Lin 1K **21**
Anderby Dr. LN6: Lin 1K **21**
Anderson LN2: Dunh 4D **4**
Anderson Cl. NG24: Bald 5F **37**
Anderson La. LN1: Lin 7F **11**
Andover Cl. LN6: Lin 6F **15**
Angelica Rd. LN1: Lin 2C **16**
Anglesey Cl. LN6: Lin 7G **15**
Anson Cl. LN6: Skel 2E **14**
Antrim Rd. LN5: Lin 5D **22**
Anzio Cl. LN1: Lin 6E **10**
Anzio Cres. LN1: Lin 6E **10**
Anzio Ter. LN1: Lin 6E **10**
Anzio Wlk. LN1: Lin 6E **10**
Apley Cl. LN2: Lin 5G **11**
Appian Way LN4: Brace H 5G **23**
Apple Av. NG24: Bald 6K **37**
Appleby Cl. NG24: N'wark T 7H **35**
Appleby Ho. *LN6: Lin 7K 15*
(off Carrington Dr.)
Appleby Way LN6: Lin 6F **15**
Apple Cl. LN4: H'ton 6G **19**
Apple Gth. LN5: Lin 3D **22**
Appleton Ga. NG24: N'wark T 7E **34**
Apple Tree Cl. LN4: Meth 4H **29**
NG24: N'wark T 5E **34**
Arabis Cl. LN2: Lin 5J **11**
Arboretum Av. LN2: Lin 3G **17**
Arboretum Vw. LN2: Lin 3G **17**
Arcade, The NG24: N'wark T 7D **34**
Archer Rd. LN4: Bran 3E **24**
Archer St. LN5: Lin 7D **38** (4F **17**)
Archway Dr. LN8: Wrag 4F **7**
Arden Moor Way LN6: N Hyk 7H **21**
Arlington Ct. LN4: Wash 5D **18**
Arnhem Cl. LN1: Lin 6E **10**
Arras Cl. LN1: Lin 7E **10**
Arthur St. LN5: Lin 5F **17**
Arthur Taylor St. LN1: Lin 3D **16**
Arvina Cl. LN6: N Hyk 7G **21**
Ascot Way LN6: N Hyk 7F **21**
Ashby Av. LN6: Lin 7K **15**
Ashby Cl. LN5: Wad 6D **22**
Ash Cl. LN6: Lin 6J **15**
Ashdale Cl. LN4: Meth 4G **29**
Asheridge LN4: Bran 3F **25**
Ashfield Grange LN1: Sax 2D **8**
Ashfield St. LN2: Lin 3H **17**
Ash Gro. LN3: C Will 1F **19**
LN6: N Hyk 5K **21**
Ash Holt Cl. LN3: Fis 3K **19**
Ashing La. LN2: Dunh 3F **5**
(not continuous)
Ash La. LN5: Wad 3E **26**
Ashley Ct. LN5: Lin 7D **16**
Ashlin Gro. LN1: Lin 3A **38** (2D **16**)
Ash Rd. NG24: N'wark T 4D **36**
Ashton's Ct. LN5: Lin 7B **38** (5E **16**)
Ash Tree Av. LN2: Nett 2C **12**
Ash Tree Way LN5: Bass 4C **30**
Ashworth Cl. LN6: Lin 2K **21**
NG24: N'wark T 7H **35**
Aspen Way LN6: S Hyk 7F **21**
Asterby Cl. LN2: Lin 6G **11**
Aster Cl. LN2: Lin 5J **11**
Aston Cl. LN5: Wad 2F **27**
Astral Way LN6: N Hyk 6G **21**
Astwick Rd. LN6: Lin 2A **22**
Atwater Cl. LN2: Lin 6K **11**
Atwater Ct. LN2: Lin 6K **11**
Atwater Gro. LN2: Lin 6K **11**
Aubourn Av. LN2: Lin 6F **11**
Auden Cl. LN2: Lin 1G **17**
Augustus Cl. LN6: N Hyk 7H **21**
Austen Wlk. LN2: Lin 7J **11**
Autumn Cft. Rd. NG24: N'wark T 6H **35**
Avalon Ct. LN1: Lin 7F **11**
Avenue, The LN1: Lin 4A **38** (3E **16**)
LN4: Noct 6B **28**
LN6: Swin 4A **26**
NG24: N'wark T 1F **37**
Avenue Ter. LN1: Lin 3A **38** (2E **16**)
Avocet Cl. LN6: Lin 6H **15**
Avon Cl. LN6: N Hyk 5A **22**
Avondale LN6: N Hyk 6G **21**
Avondale St. LN2: Lin 3G **17**
Ayam Cl. LN2: Welt 2C **4**
Aylesby Cl. LN1: Lin 5F **11**
Aynsley Cl. LN6: Lin 1G **21**
Aynsley Rd. LN6: Lin 1F **21**
Azalea Rd. LN2: Lin 5J **11**

B

Back La. LN2: Scot 7H **5**
LN4: Duns 1F **29**
LN4: H'ton 7G **19**
LN5: Carl M 6B **30**
Badgers Cl. LN6: Skel 1E **14**
Badgers Oak LN5: Bass 2D **30**
Baggholme Rd. LN2: Lin 5E **38** (3G **17**)
Baildon Cres. LN6: N Hyk 4A **22**
Bailey Rd. NG24: N'wark T 3D **36**
Bailgate LN1: Lin 2C **38** (2F **17**)
Baines Av. NG24: New B 4H **37**
Bain St. LN1: Lin 5D **10**
Bakehouse Ct LN3: L'worth 4C **6**
Baker Cres. LN6: Lin 7J **15**
Bakers La. LN5: Bass 3C **30**
Bakewell Cl. NG24: New B 5G **37**
Bakewell Ct. NG24: New B 5G **37**
Bakewell Ho. NG24: Bald 5G **37**
Bakewell M. LN6: N Hyk 6K **21**
BALDERTON **4H 37**
Balderton Ga. NG24: N'wark T 7E **34**
Balderton La. NG24: Codd 2K **37**
Ballerini Way LN1: Sax 3G **9**
Balmoral Cl. LN8: Wrag 4G **7**
Balmoral Dr. NG24: N'wark T 7J **35**
Balmoral Ho. LN2: Lin 5H **11**
Bamford Cl. LN6: N Hyk 5J **21**
Bancroft Rd. NG24: N'wark T 2F **37**
Bangor Cl. LN5: Lin 4C **22**
Banks Lodge *LN6: Lin 3D 16*
(within The Pavilions Student Village)
Bank St. LN2: Lin 5C **38** (3F **17**)
Baptist La. NG23: Coll 4G **33**
Bardney Cl. LN6: Lin 1K **21**
Bardney Rd. LN4: Wash 5K **19**
LN8: Wrag 5F **7**
Barff Rd. LN4: Pott 2B **28**
Barfields La. LN2: Scot 3H **13**
LN3: Scot 3H **13**
Bar Gate NG24: N'wark T 6D **34**
Bargate LN5: Lin 6E **16**
Barker's Ct. LN5: Lin 5D **38**
Barkstone Cl. NG24: Bald 5G **37**
Barkston Gdns. LN2: Lin 6H **11**
Bar La. LN5: Wad 3F **27**
Barley Cl. LN4: Meth 5G **29**
Barleyfield Cl. LN4: H'ton 6E **18**
Barley Way NG24: N'wark T 3F **35**
BARLINGS **7E 6**
Barlings Cl. LN3: L'worth 5C **6**
LN6: Lin 7K **15**
Barlings La. LN3: Barl, L'worth 5C **6**
BARNBY CROSSING **2G 37**
Barnby Ga. NG24: N'wark T 7E **34**
Barnby Rd.
NG24: Bald, Barn W, N'wark T 1F **37**
Barnes La. LN5: Well 6H **31**
Barnes Wallis Ct. LN2: Welt 1C **4**
Barnfield Rd. NG23: Coll 3J **33**
Barn Owl Way LN4: Wash 5D **18**
Barratt's Cl. LN2: Lin 1E **38** (1G **17**)
Barrett Gro. LN2: Dunh 3E **4**
Barrons Cl. LN3: C Will 6G **13**
Barrows Ga. NG24: N'wark T 4F **35**
BASSINGHAM **2D 30**
Bassingham Cres. LN2: Lin 6F **11**
Bassingham Rd. LN5: Carl M 6C **30**
LN5: Thurl 1C **30**
Bathley La. NG23: Bath, Lit C 1A **34**
(not continuous)
NG23: N Mus 4A **32**
Bath Rd. LN4: Brace H 3H **23**
Bathurst St. LN2: Lin 2K **17**
Battersby Cl. LN5: Bass 2D **30**
Bawtry Cl. LN6: Lin 6F **15**
Bayford Dr. NG24: N'wark T 1J **37**
Bayons Ho. *LN6: Lin 7K 15*
(off Carrington Dr.)
Baywood Cl. LN6: Lin 5G **15**
Beacon Hgts. NG24: N'wark T 7H **35**
Beacon Hill Conservation Pk. **6G 35**
Beacon Hill Rd. NG24: N'wark T 7E **34**
Beaconsfield Dr. NG24: Codd 5K **35**
Beaconsfield Gro. NG24: Codd 4K **35**
Beacon Ter. NG24: N'wark T 7E **34**
Beacon Way NG24: N'wark T 7H **35**
Beast Mkt. Hill NG24: N'wark T 6D **34**
Beaufort Cl. LN2: Lin 5K **11**
Beaufort Rd. LN2: Lin 5K **11**
BEAUMOND HOUSE COMMUNITY HOSPICE **1D 36**
Beaumont Fee LN1: Lin 4B **38** (3E **16**)
(not continuous)
Beaumont Wlk. NG24: N'wark T 5F **35**
Beaver Cl. LN6: Skel 1E **14**
Becke Cl. LN3: C Will 1G **19**
Becket Cl. LN4: Wash 5F **19**
Beckhall LN2: Welt 2C **4**
Beckhead Pk. LN6: N Hyk 7G **21**
Beck Hill LN3: Ree 5H **13**
Beckingham Rd. NG24: Codd 6K **35**
Beck La. LN2: Dunh 3F **5**
LN4: H'ton 6G **19**
Beckside LN2: Nett 2B **12**
LN6: N Hyk 7K **21**
Bede Ho. Ct. NG24: N'wark T 7E **34**
Bede Ho. La. NG24: N'wark T 7E **34**
Bedford St. LN1: Lin 2D **16**
Beech Av. LN2: Nett 2A **12**
NG24: N'wark T 3D **36**

Beech Cl. LN2: Dunh 4E 4
  LN2: Scot 1G 13
  LN4: Brace H 5G 23
Beech Ct. LN5: Lin 2D 22
Beech Cft. Cl. LN6: S Hyk 7F 21
Beech Rd. LN4: Bran 3C 24
Beech St. LN5: Lin 2D 22
Bee Field, The LN2: Lin 6B 12
Beeston Rd. NG24: N'wark T 2F 37
Belgrave Cl. LN4: Wash 5D 18
Belgravia Cl. LN6: Lin 4J 15
Belle Vue Rd. LN1: Lin 2A 38 (2E 16)
Belle Vue Ter. LN1: Lin 2A 38 (2E 16)
Bellflower Cl. LN2: Lin 5J 11
Bell Gro. LN6: Lin 1C 22
Bell La. NG23: Coll 4G 33
Bellmond Cl. NG24: N'wark T 3D 36
Bells Ct. LN5: Carl M 6C 30
Bell's Mdw. LN4: H'ton 7G 19
Bell St. LN5: Lin 6E 16
Bellwood Grange LN3: C Will 6G 13
Belmont St. LN2: Lin 3H 17
Belton Av. LN6: Lin 1K 21
Belton Pk. Dr. LN6: N Hyk 7K 21
Belton Sq. LN4: H'ton 7G 19
Belvedere Ho. LN2: Lin 5F 11
Belvoir Cl. LN5: Wad 6D 22
Belvoir Cres. NG24: N'wark T 2E 36
Belvoir Pl. NG24: Bald 5G 37
Belvoir Rd. NG24: Bald 5G 37
Belvoir Sq. LN4: H'ton 7G 19
Benbow Way LN1: Lin 7C 10
Bendigo Cl. LN1: Lin 6D 10
Bennington Cl. LN6: Lin 7K 15
Benson Cl. LN6: Lin 1G 21
Benson Cres. LN6: Lin 1G 21
Bentinck Rd. NG24: N'wark T 2D 36
Bentinck Sq. LN2: Lin 3H 17
Bentinck St. LN2: Lin 3H 17
Bentley Dr. LN4: Brace H 4F 23
Bentley Way LN4: Meth 4G 29
Beresford Cl. LN6: Lin 4D 16
Beresford Dr. LN2: Scot 1H 13
Berilldon Dr. LN1: Lin 6C 10
Berkeley Av. LN6: Lin 4A 22
Berkeley Cl. LN4: Wash 4D 18
Berkeley Dr. LN6: Lin 4A 22
Bernard St. LN2: Lin 3H 17
Besthorpe Rd. NG23: Best, Coll 1G 33
Beswick Cl. LN6: Lin 7H 15
Betula Gro. LN6: Lin 7H 15
Bevercotes Cl. NG24: N'wark T 2C 36
Beverley Gro. LN6: N Hyk 4K 21
Bilsby Cl. LN2: Lin 5G 11
Bilton Cl. NG24: Bald 6H 37
Binbrook Cl. LN6: Lin 7H 15
Birch Cl. LN4: Bran 3D 24
  LN6: N Hyk 5K 21
Birches, The LN6: S Hyk 7F 21
Birch Rd. NG24: New B 3G 37
BIRCHWOOD 6G 15
Birchwood Av. LN6: Lin 6G 15
Birchwood Cen. LN6: Lin 6G 15
Birchwood Community & Leisure Cen. 6G 15
Birchwood Grange LN6: Lin 5J 15
(off Meadowlake Cl.)
Birds Holt Cl. LN6: Skel 3E 14
Birkdale LN5: Lin 6D 22
Birkdale Cl. LN4: H'ton 5G 19
Bishop Alexander Ct.
  NG24: N'wark T 1C 36
Bishop Cl. LN2: Dunh 3F 5
Bishop King Ct. LN5: Lin 5F 17
BISHOP'S BRIDGE 6A 10
Bishops Ga. LN1: Lin 6E 10
Bishop's Pl. LN2: Welt 2B 4
Bishops Rd. LN2: Lin 1J 17
Bittern Way LN6: Lin 6H 15
Blackberry Cl. LN6: S Hyk 7F 21
Blackberry Way NG24: Bald 6J 37
Blackbird Way LN6: With S 6A 26
Blackbourn Cl. NG23: Coll 3J 33
Blackbourn Rd. LN6: Lin 1C 22
Blackbrook Rd. NG24: N'wark T 6H 35
Blackfriars Cl. LN2: Lin 7A 12
Blackfriars Rd. LN2: Lin 7A 12
Blackfriars Wlk. LN2: Lin 7A 12
Black Horse Cl. LN5: S Hyk 7E 20
Black La. LN6: Dodd, Whi 1A 20
Black's Cl. LN5: Wad 3F 27
Blacksmith Ct. LN4: Meth 4H 29

Blacksmith La. LN4: H'ton 6G 19
  LN5: Booth G 1H 31
  LN5: Harm 7E 26
  LN6: T Hill 7B 20
Blacksmith M. LN5: Nav 4J 31
Blacksmith Rd. LN3: Fis 1K 19
Blacksmith Row LN5: Bass 2D 30
Blacksmith's Grn. LN3: C Will 7G 13
Blacksmith's La. LN5: Well 6H 31
Blackthorn Cl. LN2: Lin 5J 11
Blackthorn Ct. LN2: Lin 7F 21
Blackthorne Cl. NG24: New B 3G 37
Blackthorn La. LN3: C Will 6G 13
Blackthorn Way LN4: Wash 5K 19
BLANKNEY 7H 29
Blankney Cl. LN1: Sax 2D 8
Blankney Cres. LN2: Lin 5F 11
Blankney Golf Course 7H 29
Blatherwick Rd. NG24: N'wark T 7H 35
Blenheim Cl. LN6: Skel 2D 14
Blenheim Rd. LN1: Lin 2D 16
Blenheim Sq. LN1: Lin 6E 10
Blenkin Hall LN1: Lin 7F 11
Blind La. LN5: Wad 3E 26
Bloxholm La. LN4: Brace H 5H 23
Bluebell Cl. LN6: Lin 5C 22
Bluebell Ct. LN4: Brace H 5G 23
Bluebell Wlk. LN6: With S 6B 26
  NG24: N'wark T 6H 35
(not continuous)
Blyton Cl. LN6: Lin 7G 15
Blyton Gro. LN6: Lin 7G 15
Blyton Rd. LN6: Lin 7G 15
BMI THE LINCOLN HOSPITAL 1D 38 (1F 17)
Boar La. NG24: N'wark T 7D 34
Bobbin La. LN2: Lin 7A 12
Bodmin Moor Cl. LN6: N Hyk 6H 21
Bolton Av. LN6: N Hyk 4A 22
Bona Cl. LN4: Meth 5H 29
Boole Cl. LN2: Lin 7G 11
BOOTHBY GRAFFOE 1H 31
Boscombe Cl. LN6: Lin 1G 21
Boswell Dr. LN6: Lin 3A 22
Boswell Gro. LN6: Lin 2K 21
Bottesford Cl. LN6: Lin 6H 15
Bottom Row NG24: N'wark T 7F 35
BOULTHAM 6D 16
Boultham Av. LN5: Lin 5E 16
BOULTHAM MOOR 7C 16
Boultham Pk. Rd. LN6: Lin 7C 16
Boundary Ct. NG24: N'wark T 1D 36
Boundary La. LN6: S Hyk 7E 20
Boundary Paddock LN5: Nav 5J 31
Boundary Rd. NG24: N'wark T 1C 36
Boundary St. LN5: Lin 1D 22
Bourne Cl. LN6: Lin 2B 22
Bowbridge La.
  NG24: New B, N'wark T 4E 36
Bowbridge Rd. NG24: N'wark T 1E 36
Bowden Dr. LN6: Lin 2A 22
Bower Caravan Site NG24: N'wark T 6C 34
Bower Ct. NG24: N'wark T 6E 34
BRACEBRIDGE 1D 22
BRACEBRIDGE HEATH 3F 23
BRACEBRIDGE LOW FIELDS 4D 22
Bracken Cl. LN6: S Hyk 6F 21
Bracken Hill La. LN4: H'ton 1G 26
Bradbury Av. LN5: Lin 5C 22
Braemar Rd. NG23: Coll 4H 33
Bramble Cl. LN2: Welt 1C 4
Bramble Ct. LN2: Nett 2D 12
  LN4: Brace H 5G 23
Brambles, The LN3: C Will 7D 12
Bramley Ct. LN6: Lin 3K 21
Brancaster Dr. LN6: Lin 6C 16
Brandon Cl. NG24: Bald 4J 37
BRANSTON 4E 24
Branston Bus. Pk. LN4: Bran 3C 24
Branston Cl. LN6: Lin 3B 22
  NG24: Wint 1H 35
Branston Community Academy Pool 2F 25
BRANSTON MOOR 3J 25
Branston Rd. LN4: Bran, H'ton 2E 24
Brantley M. LN5: Lin 2D 22
Brant Rd. LN5: Wad 3B 26
Brattleby Cres. LN2: Lin 6F 11
Brayford Ct. LN1: Lin 3A 38
Brayford Quays LN1: Lin 4A 38 (3E 16)
Brayford St. LN5: Lin 5B 38 (3E 16)
Brayford Way LN6: Lin 4A 38 (3D 16)
Brayford Wharf E. LN5: Lin 6B 38 (4E 16)
Brayford Wharf Nth. LN1: Lin 4A 38 (3E 16)

Brayland Ter. LN2: Lin 2K 17
(off Monks Rd.)
Brecon Cl. LN6: Lin 7F 15
Breedon Dr. LN1: Lin 6D 10
Brewer's Wharf NG24: N'wark T 6D 34
Brewery La. LN5: Carl M 6C 30
Brewhouse, The NG24: N'wark T 7D 34
(off Castle Brewery)
Briar Cl. LN6: Lin 5G 15
  LN6: S Hyk 7F 21
Brickyard La. LN5: Nav 3H 31
Bridge Ct. NG24: Bald 4K 37
Bridge Pl. LN1: Sax 3F 9
Bridge St. LN1: Sax 3E 8
  LN2: Nett 2B 12
  NG24: N'wark T 7D 34
Bridge Wlk. LN1: Burt W 7J 9
Bridle La. LN5: Carl M 7C 30
Bridle Way LN8: Wrag 3H 7
Bridle Way, The LN4: Noct 6B 28
Brigg Cl. LN6: Lin 1G 21
Brigg Gro. LN6: Lin 1G 21
Brigg La. LN5: Carl M 7C 30
Brigg Rd. LN2: Ris 1E 10
Brinkhall Way LN2: Welt 1C 4
Brinkle Spring La. LN4: H'ton 6J 19
Brisbane Cl. LN5: Wad 1C 26
Brisbane Ct. NG24: Bald 4H 37
Bristol Cl. NG24: Codd 6J 35
Bristol Dr. LN6: Lin 6C 16
Brittania Cl. NG24: N'wark T 7C 34
Broad Dale Cl. LN2: Scot 1H 13
Broadgate LN2: Lin 5D 38 (3F 17)
BROADHOLME 5E 8
Broadholme Rd. LN1: Sax 4E 8
Broadway LN2: Lin 7F 11
  LN4: Brace H 4G 23
  LN6: N Hyk 4K 21
Broadway Cl. LN2: Lin 7F 11
Brockenhurst Cl. LN6: Lin 7F 15
Brocklebank Cl. LN5: Bass 3D 30
Brockton Av. NG24: Farn 3A 36
Bromley Av. NG24: N'wark T 2E 36
Brooke Cl. NG24: Bald 3H 37
Brookfield Av. LN2: Nett 1C 12
Brookfield Cl. LN6: Skel 1E 14
Brooklands Cl. LN6: Lin 7G 15
  NG23: Coll 3H 33
Brooklands Way LN6: Lin 7G 15
Brook St. LN2: Lin 5D 38 (3F 17)
Broome Cl. NG24: New B 3F 37
Broomhill Cl. LN6: Lin 6G 15
Brough Cl. LN6: Lin 7G 15
Broughton Dr. NG24: N'wark T 3C 36
Broughton Gdns. LN5: Lin 4D 22
  NG24: Bald 4J 37
Broughton Rd. LN5: Carl M 6C 30
Browning Dr. LN2: Lin 6H 11
Browning Rd. NG24: Bald 3J 37
Brownlow's Hill NG24: Codd 6K 35
Brown Wood La. NG23: Thor 7A 8
Broxburn Pk. LN6: S Hyk 7E 20
Broxholme Gdns. LN2: Lin 5F 11
Broxholme La. LN1: Brox, Sax, Burt L 1J 9
  LN1: Sax 1F 9
Bruce Cl. LN2: Lin 7G 11
Bruce Rd. LN2: Lin 7G 11
Brumby Cres. LN5: Wad 2E 26
Brunel Bus. Pk. NG24: N'wark T 6F 35
Brunel Cl. NG24: N'wark T 5G 35
Brunel Dr. NG24: N'wark T 3G 35
Brunel Dr. Workshops NG24: N'wark T 3G 35
Brutus Ct. LN6: N Hyk 7G 21
Bryans Cl. NG24: Codd 5J 35
Buchanan St. LN1: Lin 5D 10
Buck Cl. LN2: Lin 7K 11
Buckfast Rd. LN1: Lin 7E 10
Buckingham Ho. LN2: Lin 5G 11
Bucknall Av. LN2: Lin 7K 15
Buddleia Dr. LN4: Bran 3D 24
Buller Cl. NG23: Coll 3J 33
Bullingham Rd. LN2: Lin 6K 11
Bullpit Rd. NG24: Bald 4H 37
Bungalows, The LN3: C Will 2C 18
Bunkers Hill LN2: Lin 7K 11
Bure Cl. LN6: Lin 4K 21
Burghley Cl. LN6: Lin 5J 15
Burghley Pk. Cl. LN6: N Hyk 6K 21
Burghley Rd. LN6: Lin 5J 15
Burghley Sq. LN4: H'ton 7G 19
Burland Ct. LN4: Bran 3E 24
  LN4: Wash 4D 18

Burneside Cl. LN2: Lin 5H 11
Burnmoor Cl. LN6: Lin 5G 15
Burns Gdns. LN2: Lin 7J 11
BURTON-BY-LINCOLN 3B 10
Burton Cliffe LN1: Lin 6D 10
Burtonfield Cl. LN3: C Will 7G 13
Burton La. End LN1: Burt W 6H 9
(not continuous)
Burton M. LN1: Lin 7E 10
LN4: Wash 5F 19
Burton Ridge LN1: Lin 6D 10
Burton Rd. LN1: Lin 1B 38 (7E 10)
BURTON WATERS 7J 9
Burton Waters Lodges LN1: Burt W 6H 9
Burwell Cl. LN2: Lin 5G 11
Butchers La. LN4: H'ton 7G 19
Butchery Ct. LN2: Lin 4C 38 (3F 17)
Buttercup Cl. NG24: New B 3G 37
Buttercup Way LN6: N Hyk 7F 21
LN6: With S 6B 26
Buttergate, The NG24: N'wark T 7D 34
(off Market Pl.)
Buttermere Cl. LN6: Lin 5H 15
Butters Cnr. LN4: Meth 5H 29
(off Townsend Way)
Buttery Cl. LN6: Lin 3K 21
Byland Cl. LN2: Lin 7A 12
Byron Av. LN2: Lin 7G 11
Byron Cl. NG24: N'wark T 2E 36
Byron Ct. NG24: Bald 5J 37

C

Cabourne Av. LN2: Lin 6H 11
Cabourne Ct. LN2: Lin 6H 11
Cade Cl. LN2: Scot 7G 5
Cadwell Cl. LN6: Lin 7G 15
Caenby St. LN1: Lin 7D 10
Caesar Rd. LN6: N Hyk 7G 21
Cafferata Way NG24: N'wark T 6G 35
Cairns Way LN5: Wad 7C 22
Caistor Cl. LN6: Lin 7G 15
Caistor Dr. LN4: Brace H 3G 23
Caistor Rd. LN6: Lin 7G 15
Calder Rd. LN6: Lin 5C 22
Cambrai Cl. LN1: Lin 6E 10
Cambrian Way LN6: N Hyk 7H 21
Cambridge Av. LN1: Lin 1D 16
Cambridge Dr. LN4: Wash 5E 18
Cambridge Mdws. NG24: N'wark T 7J 35
Camdale La. NG24: Bald 6K 37
Camdon Cl. LN5: Lin 4D 22
Cameron La. NG24: Bald 7K 37
Camp Rd. LN6: With S 6A 26
Campus Way LN1: Lin 3D 16
LN6: Lin 3D 16
Camwood Cres. LN6: Lin 5G 15
Canberra Sq. LN5: Wad 3G 27
Canberra Way LN6: Skel 2E 14
Cannon Cl. NG24: N'wark T 6J 35
Cannon Stevens Cl. NG23: Coll 4H 33
Cannon St. LN2: Lin 5E 38 (3G 17)
(not continuous)
Canon Cook Cl. LN1: Sax 1E 8
Canterbury Dr. LN4: H'ton, Wash 6F 19
Canterbury Rd. LN4: Brace H 3G 23
CANWICK 6H 17
Canwick Av. LN4: Brace H 3F 23
Canwick Hill LN4: Can 6G 17
Canwick Park Golf Course 5J 17
Canwick Rd. LN4: Wash 6D 18
LN5: Lin 7D 38 (4F 17)
(not continuous)
Canwick Rd. Trad. Est. LN5: Lin . . .7E 38 (5G 17)
Capps La. LN5: Wad 3E 26
Cardinal Cl. LN2: Lin 1K 17
Cardinal Hinsley Cl. NG24: N'wark T 4B 36
Cardyke Way LN4: Brace H 2C 16
Carholme Golf Course 4F 16
Carholme Rd. LN1: Lin 4A 38 (2C 16)
Carholme Rdbt. LN1: Lin 7A 10
Carisbrooke Cl. LN1: Lin 7E 10
Carline Rd. LN1: Lin 1A 38 (2E 16)
Carlisle Cl. LN6: N Hyk 6K 21
Carlisle Way LN4: Brace H 3H 23
Carlton Blvd. LN2: Lin 1K 17
Carlton Cen. LN2: Lin 7K 11
Carlton Cl. NG24: N'wark T 2E 36
Carlton Ferry La. NG23: Coll 3F 33
Carlton Gro. LN2: Lin 6F 11
CARLTON-LE-MOORLAND 7C 30

Carlton M. LN2: Lin 7K 11
LN4: Wash 5F 19
Carlton Rd. LN5: Bass 5C 30
NG24: N'wark T 7A 34
Carlton Sq. LN2: Lin 7K 11
Carlton St. LN1: Lin 1E 16
Carlton Wlk. LN2: Lin 6F 11
Carlyle Wlk. LN2: Lin 7H 11
Carmelita Av. NG24: Bald 6K 37
Carn Cl. LN5: Lin 5D 22
Carnall La. NG24: Bald 7K 37
Carnoustie Dr. LN6: Lin 7F 15
Caroline Rd. LN4: Meth 4H 13
Carpenters Cl. LN3: Ree 4F 7
LN8: Wrag 4F 7
Carral Cl. LN5: Lin 4C 22
Carram Cl. LN1: Lin 6C 10
Carram Way LN1: Lin 6C 10
Carrington Dr. LN6: Lin 7K 15
Carr La. LN6: Dodd 3A 14
NG23: Harby 7D 8
Carrs, The LN2: Welt 2C 4
Carr Cl. LN1: Lin 2D 16
Carr St. LN1: Lin 2D 36
Carswell Cl. NG24: N'wark T 7D 34
Carter Ga. NG24: N'wark T 7D 34
Carter's Cl. LN3: C Will 6D 12
Carters Yd. NG24: N'wark T 7D 34
(off Carter Ga.)
Cassia Grn. LN6: Lin 6G 15
Castle Brewery NG24: N'wark T 7D 34
Castle Brewery Ct.
NG24: N'wark T 7D 34
Castle Gate NG24: N'wark T 7D 34
Castlegate Cen. 2C 38 (2F 17)
Castle Hill LN1: Lin 1B 38 (2E 16)
Castle La. LN1: Lin 1B 38 (2E 16)
LN5: Booth G 2F 31
Castle Rising NG24: N'wark T 7D 34
(off Lombard St.)
Castle St. LN1: Lin 1E 16
Castle Vw. Caravan Pk. NG24: N'wark T . . .7B 34
Castle Vw. Ct. NG24: N'wark T 6D 34
Cathedral Hgts. LN4: Brace H 3G 23
Cathedral St. LN2: Lin 4D 38 (2F 17)
Cathedral Vw. Ct. LN2: Lin 4F 37
Catkin Way NG24: New B 4J 31
Cat Wlk. LN5: Nav 4J 31
Cavalier Building, The NG24: N'wark T 5E 34
(off North Gate)
Cavalry Ct. LN4: Meth 4J 29
Cavendish Av. NG24: N'wark T 2E 36
Cavendish M. LN4: Wash 5F 19
Cawthorne Cl. NG23: Coll 3J 33
Caythorpe Ho. LN6: Lin 7K 15
Cecil M. LN1: Lin 1C 38 (1F 17)
Cecil St. LN1: Lin 1B 38 (1E 16)
Cedar Av. LN3: C Will 1F 19
LN5: Lin 3D 22
NG24: N'wark T 4F 35
Cedar Cl. LN2: Scot 1H 13
LN5: Wad 7C 22
Cemetery Rd. LN8: Wrag 4H 7
Centaur Rd. LN6: Lin 4D 16
Centenary Cl. NG24: New B 4G 37
Central Mkt. LN5: Lin 5C 38 (3F 17)
Centurion Cl. LN5: Nav 4K 31
Century La. LN1: Sax 1E 8
Century St. NG24: N'wark T 7E 34
Chain La. NG24: N'wark T 7D 34
Chalet Caravan Site, The NG23: Bath 4A 32
Chalfonts, The LN4: Bran 3F 25
Chalgrove Way LN6: Lin 5C 6
Chamberlains Cl. LN3: L'worth 2B 4
Chancel Ct. LN2: Welt 2B 4
Chancery Cl. LN6: Lin 2B 22
Chantry Cl. NG24: N'wark T 3D 36
Chapel Cl. LN3: Ree 5H 13
Chapel Jetty LN5: Bass 3D 30
Chapel La. LN1: Lin 1B 38 (1E 16)
LN2: Nett 2B 12
LN2: Welt 2B 4
LN4: Bran 4E 24
LN4: Duns 2G 29
LN4: H'ton 7F 19
LN5: Harm 7E 26
LN5: Nav 4J 31
LN6: N Hyk 7K 21
NG23: N Mus 3C 32
NG24: Wint 1G 35
Chapel Rd. LN3: Fis 1K 19
LN4: Meth 4E 24
Chapel Wlk. LN2: Scot 7H 5

Chapel Yd. LN1: Sax 3E 8
LN4: Bran 4E 24
Chaplin Cl. LN4: Meth 5J 29
Chaplin St. LN5: Lin 7B 38 (4E 16)
Chapter Cl. LN2: Welt 1B 4
Charles St. LN5: Lin 7D 38 (4F 17)
NG24: N'wark T 1F 37
Charles St. W. LN1: Lin 2D 16
Charlesworth Ho. LN6: Lin 3D 16
(within The Pavilions Student Village)
Charlesworth St. LN1: Lin 3D 16
Charlotte Cl. NG24: N'wark T 7E 34
Chartridge LN4: Bran 3F 25
Chase, The LN4: Meth 3H 29
Chatham St. NG24: N'wark T 1D 36
Chatsworth Cl. LN2: Lin 5J 11
Chatsworth Dr. LN6: N Hyk 5J 21
Chatsworth Rd. NG24: N'wark T 3D 36
Chatterton Av. LN1: Lin 5E 10
Chaucer Dr. LN2: Lin 7J 11
Chaucer Rd. NG24: Bald 4J 37
Checkpoint Cl. LN6: Lin 1F 21
Chedburgh Cl. LN6: Lin 1F 21
Chedworth Cl. LN6: Lin 6K 11
Chedworth Rd. LN6: Lin 6K 11
Chelmer Cl. LN6: Lin 3K 21
Chelmsford St. LN5: Lin 7C 38 (4F 17)
Chelsea Cl. LN6: Lin 4H 15
Cheriton Cl. LN5: Lin 7D 38
Cherry Av. LN4: Bran 3D 24
Cherry Blossom Ct.
LN6: Lin 6F 15
Cherry Gro. LN6: Lin 6A 16
Cherry Holt LN3: C Will 1G 19
NG24: N'wark T 3D 36
Cherry Tree Cl. LN6: N Hyk 5K 21
Cherry Tree La. LN2: Nett 2A 12
Cherry Tree Way LN4: Meth 4G 29
CHERRY WILLINGHAM 7G 13
Cheshire Cl. LN4: Bran 3E 24
Cheshire La. LN6: With S 5C 26
Cheshire Rd. LN6: Lin 1E 20
Chesney Rd. LN2: Lin 6K 11
Chester Cl. LN4: Wash 5F 19
Chester Pl. NG24: N'wark T 1C 36
Chestnut Av. NG24: N'wark T 3F 35
Chestnut Cl. LN2: Scot 1H 13
LN4: Meth 3H 29
Chestnut Copse NG24: New B 2F 37
Chestnut Cres. LN5: Bass 2D 30
Chestnut Dr. LN2: Scot 1H 13
Chestnut Gro. LN5: Wad 6C 22
Chestnut Rd. LN6: N Hyk 5K 21
Chestnuts, The LN2: Nett 1B 12
Chestnut St. LN1: Lin 1B 38 (1E 16)
Cheviot Cl. LN6: N Hyk 7J 21
Cheviot St. LN2: Lin 4E 38 (3G 17)
Chichester Rd. LN4: Brace H 3G 23
Chieftain Way LN6: Lin 6C 16
Chiltern Rd. LN5: Lin 4D 22
Chiltern Way LN6: N Hyk 7J 21
Chippendale Cl. LN6: Lin 1H 21
Chippendale Rd. LN6: Lin 1H 21
Chivenor Cl. LN6: Lin 5F 15
Christopher Cres. NG24: New B 4G 37
Christ's Hospital Ter.
LN2: Lin 3C 38 (2F 17)
Church Cl. LN2: Scot 1G 13
Church Dr. LN6: Lin 5D 16
Church Hill LN4: Wash 4D 18
Churchill Av. LN4: Brace H 3F 23
Churchill Cl. LN5: Nav 4J 31
Churchill Dr. NG24: N'wark T 3C 36
Church La. LN1: Sax 2E 8
LN2: Lin 1C 38 (1F 17)
LN2: Scot 1G 13
LN2: Welt 2C 4
LN3: C Will 1G 19
LN3: Ree 5H 13
LN4: Meth 5J 29
LN4: Pott 2A 28
LN5: Carl M 7C 30
LN5: Harm 7E 26
LN5: Nav 4H 31
LN5: Wad 3E 26
NG23: Coll 3H 33
NG23: N Mus, S Mus 7B 32
NG24: Bald 5J 37
Church Rd. LN1: Sax 2E 8
LN4: Bran 4E 24
LN6: Skel 2E 14
Church Row NG23: N Mus 4C 32

Church St. LN2: Nett 2B 12
  LN2: Scot 7G 5
  LN5: Carl M 7C 30
  LN8: Wrag 3G 7
  NG23: Coll 5G 33
  NG24: N'wark T 7D 34
Church Vw. LN2: Nett 2B 12
  NG24: Bald 5H 37
Church Vw. Cres. LN3: Fis 3K 19
Church Wlk. LN4: Meth 5H 29
  (not continuous)
  LN5: Harm 7E 26
  NG24: N'wark T 7D 34
Cirencester Cl. LN6: N Hyk 7H 21
City Crematorium, The LN4: Lin 5H 17
City Sports Cen. 7A 16
City Sq. Cen. LN5: Lin 5C 38 (3F 17)
Clara Ter. LN1: Lin 3B 38 (2E 16)
Clare Cl. LN5: Lin 4D 22
Claremont St. LN2: Lin 3G 17
Clarence Ho. LN2: Lin 6G 11
Clarence St. LN1: Lin 7E 10
Clarendon Ct. LN4: Wash 5D 18
Clarendon Gdns. LN1: Lin 5E 10
Clarendon Vw. LN1: Lin 5E 10
Claricoates Dr. NG24: Codd 5J 35
Clarina St. LN2: Lin 3H 17
Clark Cres. LN2: Lin 6J 11
Clarke Av. LN4: H'ton 7G 19
  NG24: N'wark T 3C 36
Clarke Rd. LN2: Lin 3J 21
  LN6: N Hyk 7J 21
Clarks La. NG24: N'wark T 5F 35
Clasketgate LN2: Lin 4C 38 (3F 17)
Claudius Rd. LN6: N Hyk 7H 21
Clay La. LN5: Bass 4A 30
  LN5: Carl M 7A 30
  LN6: T Hill 7A 20
  NG24: N'wark T 1F 37
Clayton Cl. NG24: N'wark T 2E 36
Clayton Ho. LN6: Lin 3D 16
  (within The Pavilions Student Village)
Clayton Rd. LN5: Lin 1D 22
Clematis App. LN6: Lin 6G 15
Clematis Cl. LN4: Bran 3D 24
Clement Av. NG24: Bald 5J 37
Clement Cl. LN4: Bran 4F 25
Cleveland Av. LN6: N Hyk 7H 21
Cleveland Sq. NG24: N'wark T 2D 36
Cliff Av. LN2: Nett 2A 12
Cliffe Ct. LN2: Welt 2C 4
Cliff La. LN4: Wash 6D 18
Cliff Nook La. NG24: N'wark T 6E 34
Cliff Rd. LN2: Welt 2B 4
  LN5: Well 7G 31
Cliffside LN5: Well 6J 31
Clifton Cres. NG24: N'wark T 4G 35
Clifton Ho. NG24: N'wark T 4D 36
Clifton St. LN5: Lin 7D 38 (4G 17)
Clint La. LN5: Nav 4J 31
Clinton Arms Ct. NG24: N'wark T 7D 34
  (off St Mark's Pl.)
Clinton Ho. LN6: Lin 3D 16
  (off Picton St.)
Clinton St. NG24: N'wark T 7D 34
Clipsham Cl. NG24: Bald 3J 37
Clive Av. LN6: Lin 6C 16
Cloisters, The LN2: Lin 2E 38
  LN2: Welt 1B 4
Close, The LN3: Fis 1K 19
  LN4: Brace H 4G 23
  NG24: N'wark T 7E 34
Clover Gdns. NG24: N'wark T 6H 35
Clover Rd. LN4: Brace H 5G 23
Club Ct. NG24: Bald 4H 37
Cludd Av. NG24: N'wark T 7J 35
Clumber Av. NG24: N'wark T 2E 36
Clumber St. LN5: Lin 7E 16
Coach M. LN5: Wad 3F 27
Coalport Cl. LN6: Lin 7H 15
Cockburn Way LN5: Harm 7E 26
CODDINGTON 6K 35
Coddington Rd. NG24: Bald 4K 37
Coging Cl. NG24: New B 5G 37
Colchester M. LN6: N Hyk 7H 21
Coleby St. LN2: Lin 3H 17
Colegrave St. LN5: Lin 7E 16
Coleman Av. NG24: New B 4F 37
Colenso Ter. LN1: Lin 2D 16
Coleraine Cl. LN5: Lin 5D 22
Coleridge Gdns. LN2: Lin 6J 11
Coleridge Grn. LN2: Lin 6J 11

Coleridge Rd. NG24: Bald 3J 37
Collection, The: Art & Archaeology in Lincolnshire 3C 38 (3F 17)
College Cl. LN1: Lin 7F 11
  NG24: N'wark T 3B 36
COLLINGHAM 4G 33
Collingham Station (Rail) 4J 33
Collingwood LN6: N Hyk 7J 21
Collinson La. NG24: Bald 7J 37
Collis Cl. NG24: N'wark T 7H 35
Colne Cl. LN6: Lin 4K 21
Coney Grn. NG23: Coll 7H 33
Coningsby Cres. LN4: Brace H 2F 23
Coningsby St. LN2: Lin 5E 38 (3G 17)
Coniston Dr. LN6: N Hyk 5A 22
Connaught Ter. LN5: Lin 2D 22
Constable Av. LN6: Lin 2A 22
Constable Cl. LN6: Lin 2A 22
Constance Av. LN6: Lin 3J 21
Conway Dr. LN6: N Hyk 5B 22
Coopers Cl. LN2: Nett 1B 12
Coopers Holt Cl. LN6: Skel 3E 14
Coopers Yd. NG24: N'wark T 7C 34
Copper Beech Cl. LN6: S Hyk 7F 21
Cordage Ct. LN1: Lin 3B 38 (2E 16)
Cormack La. NG24: Bald 7K 37
Corn Cl. LN3: Fis 3K 19
Cornflower Way LN6: N Hyk 7F 21
Cornhill LN5: Lin 5C 38 (3F 17)
Cornhill Mkt. LN5: Lin 5C 38
Cornus Cl. LN4: Bran 3E 24
Cornwall Ho. LN2: Lin 6G 11
Cornwallis Rd. LN3: Lin 2K 17
Cornwood Cl. LN2: Lin 6B 12
Coronation St. NG24: New B 3G 37
Corporation St. LN1: Lin 4C 38 (3E 16)
  LN2: Lin 4C 38 (3F 17)
Correen Cl. LN5: Lin 5D 22
Cosford Cl. LN6: Lin 6F 15
Cosgrove Cl. LN6: Lin 1A 22
Cotham La. NG24: Hawt 6B 36
Cotman Rd. LN6: Lin 1A 22
Cotman Wlk. LN6: Lin 1A 22
Cotswold Cl. LN6: N Hyk 7J 21
Cottage Cl. NG24: Bald 6H 37
Cottage La. LN6: Lin 3B 22
  NG23: Coll 7G 33
Cottage Paddock, The LN6: Lin 5D 16
Cottesford Pl. LN2: Lin 1C 38 (1F 17)
Cottesmore Rd. LN6: Lin 1G 21
Cottingham Ct. LN2: Dunh 2E 4
Cottingham Dr. LN2: Lin 7H 11
Cotton Smith Way LN2: Nett 1B 12
Coulson Rd. LN6: Lin 5D 16
Coult Av. LN6: N Hyk 7J 21
County Court
  Lincoln 7C 38 (4F 17)
Coupland Cl. LN5: Wad 4F 27
Court 2 LN6: Lin 3C 16
Court 3 LN6: Lin 3D 16
Court 4 LN6: Lin 3D 16
Court 13 LN6: Lin 3D 16
Court 14 LN6: Lin 3D 16
Court 15 LN6: Lin 3D 16
Court 16 LN6: Lin 3D 16
Court 17 LN6: Lin 3D 16
Courtfield Cl. LN2: Scot 1H 13
Courtyard, The LN5: Lin 7D 38
  NG24: N'wark T 7D 34
  (off Castle Brewery)
Cow La. NG24: N'wark T 6D 34
Cowpaddle La. LN4: Wash 4J 19
Cowper Dr. LN2: Lin 6J 11
Crab La. NG23: N Mus 5C 32
Cranbourne Chase LN6: N Hyk 7H 21
Cranbourne M. LN4: Wash 5F 19
Crane Gro. LN6: Lin 7C 16
Crankley La. NG24: N'wark T 3B 34
Cranmer Rd. NG24: N'wark T 3D 36
Cranwell Cl. NG24: N'wark T 6H 35
Cranwell St. LN5: Lin 5E 16
Craven Cl. LN5: Lin 6D 16
  (off Craven St.)
Craven St. LN5: Lin 6D 16
Craypool La. LN2: Scot 7H 5
Crees La. NG24: Farn, N'wark T 2A 36
Crescent, The LN2: Nett 1B 12
  LN3: Fis 3K 19
  LN4: Brace H 4G 23
  LN8: Wrag 4H 7
  NG24: N'wark T 2E 36
Crescent Cl. LN2: Nett 1C 12

Crescent M. LN5: Harm 7E 26
Cresta Cl. LN6: N Hyk 6H 21
Crew Rd. NG23: Coll 3J 33
Croft, The LN2: Nett 2C 12
  NG24: N'wark T 7E 34
Croft La. LN3: C Will 6G 13
  LN5: Bass 2D 30
Crofton Cl. LN3: Lin 2K 17
Crofton Dr. LN3: Lin 2K 17
Crofton Rd. LN3: Lin 2K 17
Croft St. LN2: Lin 4D 38 (3G 17)
Cromer Cl. LN6: N Hyk 6A 22
Cromwell Cl. LN4: Wash 4C 18
Cromwell Rd. NG24: N'wark T 1F 37
Cromwell St. LN2: Lin 3H 17
Crossfield Cl. LN5: Nav 5J 31
Crossings, The NG24: N'wark T 7F 35
Cross La. LN6: N Hyk 7K 21
  NG23: Coll 3J 33
  NG24: Bald 7G 37
Cross o'Cliff Cl. LN5: Lin 1E 22
Cross o'Cliff Hill LN5: Brace H, Lin 7E 16
Cross Spencer St. LN5: Lin 6E 16
Cross St. LN2: Nett 2B 12
  LN4: Pott 2A 28
  LN5: Lin 7C 38 (5F 17)
  NG24: N'wark T 7E 34
Crowland Dr. LN5: Lin 7K 15
Crow La. NG23: S Mus 6A 32
Crown Cl. NG23: Coll 3H 33
Crown Court
  Lincoln 2B 38 (2E 16)
Crown Mill Cott. LN5: Lin 5E 16
Crown St. NG24: N'wark T 1D 36
Crow Pk. LN5: S Hyk 7E 20
Croxton Dr. LN6: Lin 1K 21
Crusader Rd. LN5: Lin 5C 16
Cuckoo Wlk. LN6: With S 6A 26
Cullen Cl. NG24: N'wark T 6C 34
Cullin Cl. LN5: Lin 5D 22
Cumberland Av. LN5: Well 6H 31
Cumberland Gap LN5: Well 6H 31
Curle Av. LN2: Lin 1G 17
Currie Rd. NG24: N'wark T 5E 34
Curtis Cl. NG23: Coll 3H 33
Curtis Dr. LN4: H'ton 6F 19
Curtois Cl. LN4: Bran 4E 24
Curzon M. LN4: Wash 5F 19
Cuthberts Yd. LN1: Lin 1B 38
Cydonia App. LN6: Lin 6G 15

D

D'Aincourt Pk. LN4: Bran 3C 24
Dalderby Cres. LN2: Nett 2A 12
Dale Av. LN3: C Will 7G 13
Dale Cres. NG24: Bald 6J 37
Dales, The LN2: Nett 2B 12
Dale St. LN5: Lin 4H 17
Dale Vw. Est. LN6: N Hyk 5A 22
Daleview Mdws. LN6: N Hyk 6A 22
Dale Way NG24: Bald 6K 37
Dalewood LN5: Lin 5D 22
Dane Cl. LN4: Meth 5G 29
Danes Cotts. LN2: Lin 3C 38
Danes Courtyard LN2: Lin 3C 38
Danesgate LN2: Lin 3C 38 (2F 17)
Danes Ter. LN2: Lin 3C 38 (2F 17)
  (not continuous)
Daniel Cres. LN4: H'ton 5F 19
Daniel Gdns. LN4: H'ton 6F 19
Dankerwood Rd. LN6: S Hyk 7E 20
Daphne Cl. LN4: Bran 3E 24
Dart Av. LN6: N Hyk 5A 22
Darwin Cl. LN5: Wad 1D 26
Darwin Ct. LN2: Lin 1H 17
Daubeney Av. LN1: Sax 3F 9
David Av. LN1: Lin 5D 10
David Lloyd Leisure
  Lincoln 6H 9
Davy's La. LN4: Brace H 4G 23
Dawson Cl. LN6: Lin 1K 21
Dawsons La. LN3: Ree 5H 13
Deacon Bus. Pk. LN2: Lin 1J 17
Deacon Rd. LN2: Lin 1J 17
Deane Cl. NG23: Coll 3H 33
Deane Wlk. LN2: Dunh 3D 4
Dean Rd. LN2: Lin 1J 17
Deans Leigh LN1: Lin 5E 10
Deansway LN4: Bran 2C 24
De Caldwell Dr. NG24: N'wark T 2C 36

Deeke Rd.—Fen Vw.

Deeke Rd. NG24: Bald 6K 37
Deepdale Ent. Pk. LN2: Nett 1A 12
Deepdale La. LN2: Nett 1A 12
Dees, The LN6: Dodd 6C 14
Deevon Farm Cl. NG24: N'wark T 1B 36
De Havilland Way NG24: N'wark T 2A 36
Dellfield Av. LN6: Lin 5G 15
Dellfield Cl. LN6: Lin 4G 15
Dellfield Ct. LN6: Lin 5G 15
Deloraine Ct. LN2: Lin 2C 38 (2F 17)
LN4: Wash 4D 18
Delph Rd. LN6: N Hyk 7K 21
Denbigh Ct. NG23: Coll 3H 33
Denby Dale Cl. LN6: Lin 4G 15
Dene, The LN2: Nett 1B 12
LN6: Skel 3F 15
Dene Cl. LN6: Skel 3F 15
Denefield LN6: Skel 3F 15
Dene Rd. LN6: Skel 3F 15
Dennis Brown Ct. LN1: Sax 3F 9
Denton Cl. NG24: Bald 5G 37
Denton Ho. LN6: Lin 6K 15
Denzlingen Cl. LN6: N Hyk 6H 21
Depot St. LN1: Lin 4A 38 (3D 16)
Depot Yd. *NG24: N'wark T* *6D 34*
(off Slaughter Ho. La.)
Derby St. LN5: Lin 6E 16
Derek Miller Ct. LN1: Lin 4A 38 (3E 16)
Derwent Cl. LN6: N Hyk 5A 22
Derwent Ct. NG24: Bald 5H 37
Derwent St. LN1: Lin 2C 16
Derwent Way NG24: N'wark T 5F 35
Devon Rd. NG24: N'wark T 2C 36
Devon St. LN2: Lin 3J 17
De Wint Av. LN6: Lin 2A 22
De Wint Cl. LN4: Meth 4H 29
LN6: Lin 2B 22
De Wint Ct. LN6: Lin 2B 22
De Wint Pl. LN6: Lin 2B 22
Dickinson Way NG23: N Mus 3C 32
Digby Cl. LN6: Lin 7G 15
Dixon Cl. LN6: Lin 5D 16
Dixon Ct. LN6: Lin 5D 16
Dixon St. LN5: Lin 5C 16
LN6: Lin 5C 16
Dixon Way LN6: Lin 6D 16
Dixon Way Trad. Est. LN6: Lin 5D 16
Dobsons Quay NG24: N'wark T 6D 34
DODDINGTON 5A 14
Doddington Av. LN6: Lin 3A 22
Doddington Hall & Gardens 5A 14
DODDINGTON PARK 1G 21
Doddington Rd. LN6: Lin 1F 21
LN6: Whi 2A 20
Doddington Rdbt. LN6: Lin 1E 20
Doe Cl. LN6: With S 6A 26
Doncaster Gdns. LN5: Nav 5J 31
Dorchester Way LN6: N Hyk 7H 21
Dore Av. LN6: N Hyk 5J 21
Dorewood Ct. NG24: Bald 4J 37
Dorner Av. NG24: N'wark T 1B 36
Dorothy Av. LN4: Brace H 4G 23
Dorrigan Cl. LN1: Lin 6C 10
Dorset St. LN2: Lin 3J 17
Doughty's Ct. LN5: Lin 5D 38
Doulton Cl. LN6: Lin 7H 15
Dovecote Dr. LN2: Welt 1E 4
Dove Dale LN6: N Hyk 5K 21
Dovedale Ter. NG24: Bald 6J 37
Dowding M. LN3: Lin 2A 18
Dowding Rd. LN3: Lin 2A 18
Drake Av. LN4: Wash 5D 18
Drake St. LN1: Lin 2C 16
Drill Hall 4C 38 (3F 17)
DRINSEY NOOK 5A 8
Drinsey Nook La. NG23: Thor 7A 8
Drive, The NG24: Wint 1G 35
Drove, The LN6: S Hyk 7F 21
Drove La. NG24: Codd 1J 35
(not continuous)
Drummond Gro. NG23: Coll 4H 33
Drury Ct. *LN6: Skel* *1E 14*
(off High St.)
Drury La. LN1: Lin 3B 38 (2E 16)
Drury St. LN4: Meth 5J 29
Dryden Av. LN2: Lin 7H 11
NG24: Bald 3J 37
Dunford Rd. LN5: Lin 7D 38 (4F 17)
DUNHOLME 3E 4
Dunholme Av. NG24: N'wark T 1D 36
Dunholme Cl. LN2: Welt 2D 4
Dunholme Ct. LN2: Lin 5G 11
Dunholme Rd. LN2: Scot 4F 5
LN2: Welt 1D 4
Dunkirk Rd. LN1: Lin 7D 10
Dunlop St. LN5: Lin 5F 17
Dunmore Cl. LN5: Lin 4D 22
DUNSTON 2G 29
Dunston Cl. LN2: Lin 5G 11
Dunston Fen La. LN4: Duns 1J 29
Dunston Heath La. LN4: Duns 2F 29
Dunston Rd. LN4: Duns, Meth 2H 29
Durham Cl. LN4: Brace H 3G 23
LN6: Lin 4H 15
Durham Cres. LN4: Wash 5F 19
Dykes End NG23: Coll 5H 33

E

Eagle Dr. LN2: Welt 1C 4
Eagle La. LN6: T Hill 7A 20
Eagle Rd. LN6: Whi 2A 20
Earls Dr. LN6: Lin 6D 16
Earlsfield LN4: Bran 3F 25
Earlsfield Cl. LN6: Lin 2F 21
Earp Av. NG24: N'wark T 1E 36
East Av. LN4: Brace H 4G 23
East Bight LN2: Lin 1C 38 (1F 17)
(not continuous)
Eastbourne St. LN2: Lin 3G 17
Eastbrook Rd. LN6: Lin 3A 22
Eastcliff Rd. LN2: Lin 2G 17
East Cft. LN3: C Will 6G 13
(not continuous)
Eastcroft LN1: Sax 1E 8
Eastern Ct. NG24: N'wark T 7E 34
Eastern Ter. LN5: Lin 5D 16
Eastern Ter. La. NG24: N'wark T 7E 34
Eastfield LN5: Bass 3E 30
NG23: N Mus 4C 32
Eastfield Cl. LN2: Welt 1E 4
Eastfield La. LN2: Welt 1D 4
Eastfield St. LN2: Lin 3H 17
Eastgate LN2: Lin 2C 38 (2F 17)
LN5: Bass 3D 30
Eastgate Cl. LN2: Lin 2E 38 (2G 17)
Eastholm LN2: Lin 6B 12
Eastleigh Cl. LN6: Lin 5F 15
East Liberty LN2: Lin 2J 17
East Mill Gate LN3: C Will 7G 13
Eastoft Ho. LN6: Lin 7K 15
East Rd. LN5: Nav 4J 31
East St. LN2: Nett 1B 12
Eastway LN2: Nett 2C 12
Ebony Gro. LN6: Lin 5G 15
Eccleston's Yd. *NG24: N'wark T* *7D 34*
(off Market Pl.)
Eddystone Dr. LN6: N Hyk 6A 22
Edendale Gdns. LN1: Lin 5E 10
Edendale Vw. LN1: Lin 5E 10
Edge Cl. NG23: N Mus 2C 32
Edgehill LN5: Lin 5D 22
Edgehill Dr. NG24: N'wark T 7J 35
Edinburgh Ho. LN2: Lin 6G 11
Edinburgh Sq. LN5: Wad 2G 27
Edlington Cl. LN2: Lin 5F 11
Edna St. LN5: Lin 5F 17
Edward Av. NG24: N'wark T 7C 34
Edward Barker Rd. LN4: H'ton 7G 19
Edward Jermyn Dr. NG24: N'wark T 3F 35
Edward St. LN5: Lin 6D 16
Egerton Rd. LN2: Lin 1H 17
Egret Gro. LN6: Lin 6H 15
Elder Cl. LN6: With S 6A 26
Elder St. LN5: Lin 2D 22
Eldon St. NG24: N'wark T 1D 36
Eleanor Cl. LN5: Lin 7E 16
Electric Av. LN6: With S 6A 26
Elevation Ct. LN2: Lin 3J 17
Elizabeth Av. LN6: N Hyk 6K 21
Elizabeth Rd. NG24: N'wark T 3C 36
Elk Racing Outdoor Karting Circuit 1K 35
Ellerslie Cl. NG24: N'wark T 6E 34
Ellesmere Av. LN2: Lin 2K 17
Elliott Rd. LN5: Lin 7E 38 (5G 17)
Ellis Mill 1A 38
Ellison Cl. LN2: Scot 1H 13
Ellison Ho. *LN6: Lin* *3D 16*
(within The Pavilions Student Village)
Ellisons Quay LN1: Burt W 7J 9
Ellison St. LN5: Lin 2D 22
Elm Av. LN3: C Will 1F 19
NG24: N'wark T 2F 37
Elm Cl. LN1: Sax 2F 9
LN6: N Hyk 5K 21
NG24: N'wark T 2F 37
Elmdene LN2: Scot 7H 5
Elm Dr. LN2: Scot 1H 13
Elmwood Cl. LN6: Lin 5H 15
Elsham Cl. LN6: Lin 6H 15
Elsham Cres. LN6: Lin 6H 15
Elton Cl. LN1: Lin 6C 10
NG24: Bald 5H 37
Elvin Cl. LN2: Lin 7F 11
Elvington Cl. LN6: Lin 1F 21
Elvington Rd. LN6: Lin 1F 21
Ely Cl. LN4: Brace H 3G 23
Ely St. LN1: Lin 2D 16
Emmendingen Av.
NG24: N'wark T 4F 35
Enderby Cl. LN4: Wash 4C 1
Ennerdale Cl. LN6: Lin 5H 1
Enright Cl. NG24: N'wark T 2D 3
Enterprise Pk. NG24: N'wark T 4G 3
Epsom Cl. LN6: Lin 6F 1
Epsom Rd. LN6: Lin 6F 1
Epworth Vw. LN1: Lin 5E 1
ERMINE 5G 1
Ermine Cl. LN1: Lin 5E 1
Ermine Ct. LN4: Brace H 5G 2
Ermine Dr. LN5: Nav 4K 3
Ernest Ter. LN1: Lin 1C 38 (1F 17
Escombe Vw. LN1: Lin 5D 1
Eshings, The LN2: Welt 1D
Esk Cl. LN6: Lin 3K 2
Estwaite Cl. LN6: N Hyk 5A 2
Eton Av. NG24: N'wark T 2C 3
Eton Cl. LN6: Lin 3H 1
NG24: N'wark T 2D 3
Eton Rd. LN4: Wash 5E 1
Euston Cl. LN6: Lin 4H 1
Eve Gdns. LN4: Wash 5F 1
Everest Ct. NG24: Bald 4J 3
Ewart St. LN5: Lin 1D 2
Exchange Arc. LN5: Lin 5C 3
Exchange Cl. LN6: N Hyk 3J 2
Exchange Rd. LN6: Lin 3J
Exchequer Gate 2C 38 (2F 1
Exchequer Ga. LN2: Lin 2C 38 (2F 1
Exeter Cl. LN4: Wash 5G
Exley Sq. LN2: Lin 7K
Exmoor Cl. LN6: N Hyk 6H
Eyam Way LN6: N Hyk 6K

F

Fairfax Av. NG24: N'wark T 3C
Fairfax St. LN5: Lin 1D
Fairfield Av. NG24: New B 3H
Fairfield St. LN2: Lin 3H
Fairleas LN4: Bran 3F
Fairway NG24: N'wark T 3B
Falcon Vw. LN6: Lin 6H
Faldingworth Cl. LN6: Lin 7G
Falklands Cl. LN1: Lin 5E
Falstone Av. NG24: N'wark T 2F
Far End LN5: Booth G 1H
Far La. LN5: Wad 3E
Farmers Wlk. NG24: N'wark T 3G
Farm Vw. LN2: Welt 1
Farndon La. NG24: Hawt 6A
Farndon Rd. NG24: N'wark T 2A
Farrar Cl. NG24: N'wark T 5G
Farrier Ct. LN4: Meth 4H
Farrier Rd. LN6: Lin 2F
Farrington Cl. LN6: Lin 4H
Farrington Cres. LN6: Lin 4H
Far Wharf LN1: Lin 4A 38 (3D
Favell Rd. LN4: Wash 4D
Fawsley Cl. LN2: Lin 6A
Fayid La. LN4: Noct 5C
Featherby Pl. LN5: Lin 6E
Fen La. LN1: S Car 1A
LN4: Duns 1H
LN5: Bass 1E
LN6: N Hyk 5A
NG24: Bald, Barn W 4H
Fen Rd. LN1: Burt L 6J 9 & 4
LN4: H'ton, Wash 7
LN4: Meth 4
LN4: Wash 4
Fenton Cl. NG24: N'wark T 5
Fenton Pl. LN2: Lin 3
Fen Vw. LN4: H'ton 7

Ferguson Ho. LN6: Lin 5J 15
Fern Cl. LN6: Lin .3A 22
Fern Gro. LN3: C Will 1F 19
Fernleigh Av. LN4: Brace H 5G 23
FERNWOOD 6J 37
Fernwood Bus. Pk.
   NG24: Bald 7J 37
Ferry La. LN4: Wash 4D 18
   LN6: Skel 1F 15
   NG23: N Mus .4C 32
Ferry Rd. LN3: Fis .3K 19
Ferryside LN3: Fis .3K 19
Ferryside Gdns. LN3: Fis 4K 19
Field Cl. LN2: Nett 2C 12
   LN2: Welt 1C 4
Fieldfare Cl. LN6: Lin 6H 15
Field Farm La. LN4: Meth 4J 29
Filey Cl. LN6: N Hyk 4A 22
Finch Cl. LN6: Lin .6J 15
Finch Way LN8: Wrag 4G 7
Finningley Cl. LN6: Lin 1H 21
Finningley Rd. LN6: Lin 2H 21
Firth Rd. LN5: Lin 7A 38 (4D 16)
   LN6: Lin 7A 38 (4D 16)
Fir Tree Av. LN5: Wad 7C 22
Firtree Av. LN6: Lin 5G 15
Fir Tree Cl. LN2: Scot 1G 13
Fisher Cl. NG23: Coll 3J 33
FISKERTON 1K 19
Fiskerton Dr. LN2: Lin 5F 11
Fiskerton Rd. LN3: C Will, Lin 2D 18
   LN3: Ree 5J 13
Fiskerton Rd. E. LN3: C Will 2G 19
Fitness First
   Lincoln 5D 16
Five Bells Jetty LN5: Bass 2D 30
Five Mile Bus. Pk.
   LN4: Wash 4K 19
Five Mile La. LN4: Wash 5K 19
Flavian Rd. LN2: Lin 5H 11
Flaxengate LN2: Lin 4C 38 (3F 17)
Flaxley Cl. LN2: Lin 7A 12
Flaxley Rd. LN2: Lin 7A 12
Fleet St. LN1: Lin .2C 16
Fleming Dr. NG24: N'wark T 3F 35
Fleming Ho. LN5: Lin 2D 22
Flinders Cl. LN4: Meth 4G 29
Flinders Way LN3: C Will 7D 12
Flintham Cl. LN4: Meth 4G 29
Florence St. LN2: Lin 3H 17
Folkingham Cl. LN6: Lin 6H 15
Folly La. LN4: Bran 4A 24
Fontwell Cres. LN6: Lin 2A 22
Ford Cl. NG24: Bald 6K 37
Fordham Dr. LN1: Lin 6C 10
Fordham Ho. LN6: Lin 2B 22
Foresters Ct. NG24: N'wark T 7G 35
Forge Cl. NG23: S Mus 7A 32
Forge Cotts. NG23: S Mus 7B 32
Forrington Pl. LN1: Sax 3G 9
Forster Av. NG24: N'wark T 4C 36
Forsythia Cl. LN4: Bran 3D 24
Forum, The LN6: N Hyk 4K 21
Foss Bank LN1: Lin 3D 16
Fossdyke Gdns. LN1: Sax 3F 9
Fossdyke Ho. LN1: Sax 3E 8
Fosse Ct. LN4: Brace H 5G 23
Fosse Dr. LN6: N Hyk 4K 21
Fosse Gro. LN1: Sax 3F 9
Fosse Ho. LN6: Lin 2C 22
Fosse La. LN6: T Hill 7B 20
Fosse Rd. NG24: Farn 3A 36
Foss St. LN1: Lin .3D 16
Foster Lodge LN6: Lin 3D 16
   (within The Pavilions Student Village)
Foster Rd. NG23: Coll 3H 33
Fosters Cl. LN5: Nav 4J 31
Foster's Gdns. LN4: Pott 1B 28
Foster St. LN5: Lin 7A 38 (5E 16)
Foston Cres. LN6: Lin 7K 15
Foundry Cl. NG24: N'wark T 5D 34
Fountain Ct. LN5: Lin 2D 22
Four Seasons Cl. LN2: Dunh 3E 4
Fox Covert LN2: Scot 1J 13
   LN6: S Hyk 6E 20
Fox Covert La. LN2: Dunh 1J 5
Foxfield Cl. LN6: Skel 1E 14
Foxglove Cl. NG24: New B 4G 37
Foxglove Way LN5: Lin 5C 22
Fox Hollow LN6: With S 6B 26
Foyle Cl. LN5: Lin .5D 22
Francis Hill Ct. LN2: Lin 1D 38 (1F 17)

Francis St. LN1: Lin 1F 17
   LN5: Lin 1D 22
Franklin Cl. LN4: Meth 4H 29
Franklin Way LN3: C Will 7D 12
Frank St. LN5: Lin .5E 16
Frank Swaby Ct. LN5: Lin 1E 22
Frank Wright Ct. LN2: Lin 6J 11
Frederick St. LN2: Lin 3J 17
Freeman Rd. LN6: N Hyk 4H 21
Freeschool La. LN2: Lin 5C 38 (3F 17)
Freston Ct. LN2: Welt 1B 4
Friars Cres. NG24: N'wark T 3D 36
Friars La. LN2: Lin 4D 38 (3F 17)
Friars M. LN2: Lin .4D 38
Friary Gdns. NG24: N'wark T 6E 34
Friary M. NG24: N'wark T 6E 34
Friary Rd. NG24: N'wark T 7E 34
Friary Vs. NG24: N'wark T 6E 34
Frome Cl. LN6: Lin .2H 21
Front St. LN4: Duns 2G 29
Fulbeck Ho. LN6: Lin 1B 22
Fulford Ct. LN2: Lin 1J 17
Fulmar Cl. LN6: Lin 7J 15
Fulmar Rd. LN6: Lin 6H 15
   (not continuous)
Fulmen Cl. LN1: Lin 7C 10
Fulstow Rd. LN2: Lin 5H 11
Furndown Cl. LN6: Lin 7F 15
Furrow Cl. LN2: Welt 3C 4

G

Gabriel Cres. LN2: Lin 7A 12
Gage Ct. LN2: Lin .7K 17
   (off Stark Way)
Gail Gro. LN4: H'ton 6E 18
Gainsborough Dr. NG24: N'wark T 4F 35
Gainsborough Gdns. LN6: Lin 1B 22
Gainsborough Rd. LN1: D Noo, Sax 4A 8
   NG24: Wint 2G 35
Gaitskell Way NG24: Bald 4J 37
Gala Bingo
   Lincoln 5C 38
Gamage Cl. NG24: Bald 5J 37
Garden Ct. LN1: Lin 1C 16
Gardenfield LN6: Skel 4F 15
Gardiner Av. NG24: Bald 6K 37
Garfield Cl. LN1: Lin 5D 10
Garfield Vw. LN1: Lin 5D 10
Garmston St. LN2: Lin 3C 38 (2F 17)
Garood Cl. NG24: N'wark T 2A 36
Garratt Cl. LN4: H'ton 7F 19
Garrick Cl. LN5: Lin 4D 22
Garside Vw. LN2: Lin 2K 17
Gas La. LN5: Nav 4J 31
Gateway, The NG24: N'wark T 7F 35
Gateway Cl. LN6: S Hyk 7F 35
Gaunt St. LN5: Lin 7A 38 (4E 16)
Gayton Cl. LN2: Lin 6G 11
Geneva Av. LN2: Lin 7H 11
George St. LN5: Lin 4H 17
   NG24: N'wark T 6E 34
Gerald's Cl. LN2: Lin 1H 17
Gerbera Dr. NG24: Bald 6H 35
Gerrard M. LN4: Wash 5F 19
Gibbeson St. LN5: Lin 6E 16
Gibson Cl. LN4: Bran 3E 24
Gibson Cres. NG24: New B 5G 37
Gibson Grn. LN6: With S 5C 26
Gibson Ho. LN2: Lin 5G 11
Gilbert Way NG24: Bald 6K 37
Gildesburgh Rd. LN4: Wash 5D 18
Gill Ho. NG24: N'wark T 4E 36
Gilmores La. NG24: Bald 7K 37
Gilstrap Centre, The 6D 34
Gilstrap Cl. NG24: N'wark T 7H 35
Gladstone Rd. NG24: N'wark T 2D 36
Gleanings, The LN5: Nav 4K 31
Glebe End LN4: Can 6H 17
Glebelands NG23: N Mus 5C 32
Glebe Pk. NG24: New B 2G 37
Gleedale LN6: N Hyk 5J 21
Glenarm Cres. LN5: Lin 4D 22
Glenbank Cl. LN6: Lin 4K 21
Glendon Cl. LN5: Lin 4D 22
Gleneagles Gro. LN4: H'ton 5F 19
Glentham Cl. LN6: Lin 4B 22
Glenwood Gro. LN6: Lin 5D 16
Globe Ho. LN5: Lin .7D 38
Gloucester Ho. LN4: Brace H 3G 23

Gloucester Ho. LN2: Lin 6G 11
Glovers La. NG24: Bald 4H 37
Glynn Rd. LN1: Lin .5E 10
Glynn Vw. LN1: Lin 5E 10
Godber Dr. LN4: Brace H 4F 23
Goldcrest Cl. LN6: Lin 5J 15
Goldfinch Cl. LN6: Skel 3E 14
Goldsmith Rd. NG24: Bald 3H 37
Goldsmith Wlk. LN2: Lin 6J 11
Goldson Way NG23: N Mus 5C 32
Goldstraw La. NG24: Bald 6J 37
Good La. LN1: Lin .1F 17
Goodwin Cl. NG24: N'wark T 7H 35
Goodwin La. NG24: Bald 7K 37
Goodwood Way LN6: Lin, N Hyk 4G 21
Gopher Rd. NG24: N'wark T 3D 36
Gordon Rd. LN1: Lin 2C 38 (2F 17)
Gorehall Dr. LN2: Welt 1C 4
Gorse La. LN5: Carl M 5B 30
Gorse Rd. NG24: N'wark T 3D 36
Gothic Cl. LN6: Lin .7H 15
Goxhill Cl. LN6: Lin 7H 15
Goxhill Gro. LN6: Lin 7H 15
Grace Av. LN6: Lin, N Hyk 4G 21
Grace St. LN5: Lin .5F 17
Grafton St. LN2: Lin 3H 17
Graham Cl. NG24: New B 4F 37
Grainsby Cl. LN6: Lin 2C 22
Granary Cl. LN4: Meth 5G 29
   LN5: Wad 4F 27
Granby Av. NG24: N'wark T 2E 36
Granby Dr. NG24: Bald 5H 37
Grandfield Way LN6: N Hyk 7F 21
Granely Cl. LN1: Lin 7C 10
Grange, The NG23: N Mus 3C 32
Grange Cl. LN4: Can 6H 17
Grange Ct. LN5: Carl M 6C 30
Grange Cres. LN6: Lin 4B 22
Grange Dr. LN6: Lin 4A 22
Grange La. LN2: Ris 4F 11
   LN4: Can 6H 17
   LN4: H'ton 7F 19
   NG24: New B .7F 37
Grange Rd. LN4: Brace H 5F 23
   LN4: Meth 4J 29
   NG24: N'wark T 3B 36
Granson Way LN4: Wash 4C 18
Grantavon Ho. LN5: Lin 5B 38
Grantham Rd. LN4: Brace H 7F 23
   LN5: Booth G, Nav 1H 31
   LN5: Harm, Wad 1F 27
   LN5: Nav 5J 31
Granthams, The LN2: Dunh 3D 4
Grantham St. LN2: Lin 4C 38 (3F 17)
Grasmere Way LN6: Lin 5H 15
Grassmoor Cl. LN6: N Hyk 7H 21
Graveley Cl. LN6: Lin 1F 21
Grayson Grn. LN5: Well 6J 31
Gray St. LN1: Lin 1B 38 (1E 16)
   (not continuous)
Gt. Northern Ter. LN5: Lin 7D 38 (4G 17)
Gt. Northern Way LN5: Lin 4G 17
Great Nth. Rd.
   NG23: N'wark T, N Mus, S Mus 7A 32
   NG24: Bald 7J 37
   NG24: N'wark T 5C 34
Greaves Cl. NG24: N'wark T 7H 35
Grebe Cl. LN6: N Hyk 6G 21
   NG24: New B .3G 37
Green, The LN2: Nett 2B 12
   LN2: Scot 7H 5
   LN3: Ree 5H 13
   LN4: Duns 2H 29
   LN4: Noct 6B 28
   LN4: Pott 2A 28
   LN5: Well 6H 31
   NG23: Coll 5G 33
Greenaway Ct. LN3: C Will 7G 13
Greenbank Dr. LN6: Lin 2A 22
Greenfield Cl. NG24: Codd 6J 35
Greenfields LN2: Nett 2C 12
Greenfinch Cres. LN6: With S 7A 26
Greenholme Cl. LN2: Lin 4G 11
Green La. LN1: Hard, Sax 4B 8
   LN2: Welt 3B 4
   LN3: C Will 1E 18
   LN4: Duns . . . . .6E 28 & 1K 29
   LN6: Lin 4D 16
   LN6: N Hyk 6K 21
   LN6: Skel 1F 15
   LN6: With S 6C 26
   NG23: Coll 4J 33

Green Man Rd. LN5: Nav 3J 31
Greenock Way LN6: Lin 7F 15
Green Way LN2: Scot 1H 13
Greenway LN2: Welt 1B 4
   NG24: N'wark T 3C 36
Greenwood Cl. LN5: Wad 7C 22
Greestone Mt. LN2: Lin 3D 38 (2F 17)
Greestone Pl. LN2: Lin 3D 38 (2F 17)
Greestone Stairs LN2: Lin 3D 38
Greestone Ter.
   LN2: Lin 3D 38 (2F 17)
Greetwell Cl. LN2: Lin 2H 17
Greetwell Ct. LN2: N Gre 5D 12
Greetwell Ga. LN2: Lin 2E 38 (2G 17)
Greetwell La. LN2: Lin 7B 12
   LN2: Nett 2A 12
   LN3: Lin 7B 12
Greetwell Pl. LN2: Lin 1H 17
                   (Greetwell Cl.)
   LN2: Lin 2J 17
                (Lime Kiln Way)
Greetwell Rd. LN2: Lin 2G 17
   LN3: Lin 2G 17
Gregg Hall Cl. LN6: Lin 3B 22
Gregg Hall Cres. LN6: Lin 3B 22
Gregg Hall Dr. LN6: Lin 3B 22
Gresham Cl. NG24: N'wark T 7J 35
Gresham St. LN1: Lin 2D 16
Gresley Dr. LN6: Lin 5D 16
Greyfriar's Pathway LN2: Lin 5C 38
Greyling Cl. LN1: Lin 5E 10
Greyling Vw. LN1: Lin 5E 10
Griffin's La. LN5: Wad 1D 26
Grinter Cl. LN6: N Hyk 7K 21
Grosvenor Av. LN6: Lin 4H 15
Grosvenor Ct. LN5: Lin 2D 22
Grosvenor M. LN4: Wash 5F 19
Grosvenor Rd. NG24: New B 4F 37
Grosvenor Sq. LN5: Well 6H 31
Grove, The LN2: Lin 1E 38 (1G 17)
   LN2: Welt 2C 4
Grove Cotts. NG24: N'wark T 1G 37
Grove Leisure Cen. 2G 37
Grove St. NG24: New B 3F 37
Groveview Rd. NG24: New B 3G 37
Guildhall St. LN1: Lin 5B 38 (3E 16)
   NG24: N'wark T 7E 34
Gunby Av. LN6: Lin 1K 21
Gynewell Gro. LN2: Lin 6J 11

H

Habbanya Ri. LN4: Noct 5C 28
Hackthorn Pl. LN2: Lin 5F 11
Hackthorn Rd. LN2: Welt 1D 4
Haddon Cl. LN6: Lin 5J 15
Haddon Dr. NG24: Bald 5H 37
Hadfield Rd. LN6: Lin 2A 22
Hadleigh Dr. LN6: Lin 2K 21
Hadrians Rd. LN4: Brace H 5G 23
Hadrians Wlk. LN6: N Hyk 7F 21
Haffenden Rd. LN6: Lin 7G 11
Hainton Rd. LN6: Lin 2C 22
Hale Cl. LN2: Lin 6A 12
Hales La. LN5: Nav 4K 31
Halfpenny Cl. LN2: Welt 1D 4
Halfway Ho. Rdbt. LN6: Swin 5A 26
HALFWAY HOUSES 5A 26
Halifax Cl. LN6: Skel 2E 14
Halifax Ct. NG24: Bald 7J 37
Hallam Gro. LN6: Lin 7C 16
Hall Dr. LN4: Can 6G 17
   LN6: Lin 7D 16
Hall Farm LN4: Can 6H 17
Hallfield LN5: Bass 2C 30
Hall Gdn. LN4: Can 6H 17
Halliwell Cl. NG24: N'wark T 3F 35
Hall La. LN2: Nett 1J 11
   LN4: Bran 5B 24
Halls Ct. LN4: Duns 1G 29
Hall St. LN5: Well 6H 31
Hall Wath LN5: Bass 3C 30
Hall Yd. LN4: Meth 5H 29
Halton Cl. LN6: Lin 6F 15
Hambleton Av. LN6: N Hyk 7H 21
Hamilton Gro. LN6: Skel 3F 15
Hamilton Rd. LN5: Lin 7E 16
   LN6: N Hyk .5H 21
Hampden Cl. LN6: Skel 2E 14
Hampdens Cl. NG24: Codd 5J 35
Hampden Way LN5: Wad 2G 27

Hampton M. LN1: Lin 2D 16
Hampton St. LN1: Lin 2A 38 (2D 16)
Handley Ct. NG24: N'wark T 6D 34
Hannah Cl. LN4: Bran 3E 24
Hannah Cres. LN6: With S 5B 26
Hannah Ho. LN2: Lin 5H 11
Hanover Ho. LN2: Lin 5F 11
Hansards Dr. LN8: Wrag 3G 7
Harby Cl. LN6: Lin 4B 22
   NG24: Bald .5H 37
Harcourt St. NG24: N'wark T 1F 37
Harding House Gallery 3C 38
Hardings, The LN2: Welt 1D 4
HARDWICK 1A 8
Hardwick Av. NG24: N'wark T 1D 36
Hardwick Cl. LN1: Sax 2D 8
Hardwick Pl. LN2: Lin 5G 11
Harewood Av. NG24: N'wark T 1D 36
Harewood Cres. LN6: N Hyk 5K 21
Harewood Ho. LN2: Lin 5F 11
Hargon La. NG24: Wint 1H 35
Harlaxton Cl. LN6: Lin 1G 21
Harlaxton Dr. LN6: Lin 1G 21
HARMSTON 7E 26
Harmston Cl. LN2: Lin 5G 11
Harmston Pk. LN5: Harm 7E 26
Harmston Pk. Av. LN5: Harm 7E 26
Harpswell Rd. LN2: Lin 6G 11
Harricot Cl. LN1: Lin 6C 10
Harrier Ct. LN6: Lin 6H 15
Harrington Av. LN6: Lin 6C 16
Harrington Sq. LN4: H'ton 7G 19
Harrison Pl. LN1: Lin 1B 38 (1E 16)
Harrisons Way
   NG24: N'wark T 6F 35
Harris Rd. LN5: Wad 2F 27
   LN6: Lin 1B 22
Harrisson Pl. LN6: Lin 2H 21
Harrow Cl. LN4: Wash 5E 18
Harrows, The LN7: Wash 2C 4
Hartland Av. LN6: N Hyk 6A 22
Hartley St. LN2: Lin 3J 17
HARTSHOLME .7K 15
Hartsholme Country Pk. 7J 15
Hartsholme Country Pk. Camp Site
   LN6: Lin 7K 15
Hartsholme Country Pk. Vis. Cen. 6K 15
Hartsholme Dr. LN6: Lin 6K 15
Harvard Cl. LN4: Wash 5F 19
Harvest Cl. LN4: Meth 5G 29
Harvest Dr. NG24: N'wark T 3G 35
Harvey St. LN1: Lin 3D 16
Harwich Cl. LN5: Lin 4D 22
Haslam Ho. NG24: N'wark T 4D 36
Hatchet's La. NG24: N'wark T 4E 34
Hatcliffe Gdns. LN2: Lin 5G 11
Hathersage Av. LN6: N Hyk 5J 21
Hatton Cl. LN6: Lin 7A 16
   NG23: N Mus 4C 32
Hatton Gdns. NG24: N'wark T 1E 36
Hawkshead Gro. LN2: Lin 5G 11
Hawksmoor Cl. LN6: N Hyk 6H 21
Hawthorn Av. LN3: C Will 7D 12
   LN5: Wad 6C 22
Hawthorn Chase LN2: Lin 6A 12
Hawthorn Cl. LN4: Brace H 5G 23
   LN4: H'ton 6G 19
Hawthorn Rd. LN2: Lin 6A 12
   LN3: C Will, Ree 6E 12
Hawthorns, The LN2: Nett 1D 12
Hawthorn Way LN5: Bass 2D 30
HAWTON 5B 36
Hawton La. NG24: New B 4E 36
Hawton Rd. NG24: N'wark T 4B 36
Haydor Av. LN2: Lin 5G 11
Hayside Av. NG24: Bald 5F 37
Hay Way LN8: Wrag 3G 7
Haze La. LN6: N Hyk 6G 21
Hazel Cl. LN6: S Hyk 7E 20
Hazel Gro. LN2: Welt 2B 4
   NG24: New B 3G 37
Hazel Ho. LN2: Lin 2J 17
Hazelwood Av. LN6: Lin 5G 15
Headland Way LN5: Nav 5J 31
Healey Cl. NG23: Coll 4H 33
Heath Cl. LN2: Welt 1B 4
Heathcroft LN3: C Will 1G 19
Heather Gdns. LN6: N Hyk 4J 21
Heathfield Av. LN4: Bran 4F 25
Heath La. LN2: Welt 2A 4
   LN5: Booth G 1J 31
Heathlea LN2: Scot 7G 5

Heath Rd. LN2: Dunh, Scot 6B
   LN2: Nett 1B 1
   LN4: Brace H 5F 2
   LN5: Nav 5J 3
Heaton Cl. NG24: N'wark T 7H 3
Hebden Moor Way
   LN6: N Hyk .7H 2
Hedge La. LN6: With S 7A 2
HEIGHINGTON 6G 1
Heighington Fen LN4: Wash 5K 1
Heighington Rd. LN4: Can 6H 1
Heights, The LN1: Lin 2A 38 (2E 16
Helsby Rd. LN5: Lin 3D 2
Hemplands, The NG23: Coll 3H 3
Hemswell Av. LN6: Lin 1K 2
Henley Cl. LN5: Lin 6D 1
Henley St. LN5: Lin 6D 1
Henley Way LN6: Lin 2H 2
Henlow Cl. LN6: Lin 6F 1
Henry St. LN5: Lin 5F 1
Henson Dr. LN5: Nav 5J 3
Henton Cl. NG24: Codd 5J 3
Hercules Dr. NG24: N'wark T 1F 3
Hereward St. LN1: Lin 1C 38 (1F 17
Heritage Ct. LN5: Nav 4J 3
Hermit St. LN5: Lin 7B 38 (4E 16
Heron Vw. LN6: Lin 6J 1
Heron Wlk. LN6: N Hyk 6G 2
Heron Way NG24: New B 3G 3
Herrington Av. LN2: Nett 1B 1
Hewson Rd. LN1: Lin 2C 1
Hewson's La. NG23: Coll 7H 3
Heysham Cl. LN5: Lin 4D 2
Hibaldstow Cl. LN6: Lin 7G 1
Hibaldstow Rd. LN6: Lin 7G 1
Hickory Rd. LN6: Lin 5G 1
Higgins Cl. LN6: Lin 7J 1
   NG24: N'wark T 5E 3
Highcliffe LN5: Well 6H 3
High Dike
   LN5: Booth G, Nav, Well 1K 3
   LN5: Brace H, Wad 6H 2
High Dyke LN5: Wad 1F 2
Highfield Av. LN6: Lin 1B 2
Highfield Rd. LN1: Sax 2E
Highfields LN2: Lin 1C 1
Highfields Ri. LN4: Meth 5G 2
Highfield Ter. LN6: N Hyk 5A 2
High Leas LN2: Nett 1C 1
High Mdw. LN4: Wash 4E 1
High Mdws. LN3: Fis 1K 1
High St. LN1: Sax 2E
   LN2: Lin 4C 38 (3F 17
   LN2: Nett 2B 1
   LN3: C Will 1F 1
   LN3: Fis 2K 1
   LN3: Ree 5H 1
   LN4: Bran 4E 2
   LN4: H'ton 6F 1
   LN4: Meth 4H 2
   LN4: Wash 4D 1
   LN5: Bass 3C 3
   LN5: Carl M .6C 3
   LN5: Harm 7E 2
   LN5: Lin 7B 38 (6E 16
   LN5: Nav 4J 3
   LN5: Wad 3F 2
   LN5: Well 6H 3
   LN6: Skel 1E 1
   NG23: Coll 5G 3
   NG23: Holm .4D 3
Higson Rd. LN1: Lin 6D 1
Hill, The LN6: Skel 2E 1
Hillary Way NG24: Bald 4J 3
Hillcroft LN4: Wash 4C 1
Hillcroft Bus. Pk. LN6: Lin 1B 2
Hillman Cl. LN4: Brace H 4F 2
Hillside App. LN2: Lin 3J 1
Hillside Av. LN2: Lin 3J 1
Hillside Est. LN4: Bran 3E 2
Hill Top LN5: Harm 7E 2
   LN5: Wad . . . .
Hill Vue Av. NG24: N'wark T 7F 3
Hill Vue Gdns. NG24: N'wark T 7F 3
Hine Av. NG24: N'wark T 7H 3
HMP Lincoln LN2: Lin 2J 1
Hobart Cl. LN5: Lin 3F 2
Hodson Cl. LN6: Skel 1F 1
Holdenby Cl. LN2: Lin 6A 1
Holdenby Rd. LN2: Lin 6A 1
Holden Cres. NG24: N'wark T 2D 3
Hollies Av. NG24: N'wark T 7F 3

Hollowdyke La.—Lansdowne Rd.

Hollowdyke La. NG24: Bald .7K **37**
(Great Nth. Rd.)
NG24: Bald .5K **37**
(Spring La.)
Holly Cl. LN3: C Will .1G **19**
LN5: Lin .2D **22**
Holly Ct. NG24: N'wark T .6H **35**
Holly M. NG24: New B .3G **37**
Holly St. LN5: Lin .2D **22**
Hollywell Rd. LN5: Wad .6C **22**
HOLME .3D **32**
Holme Cl. LN6: T Hill .7C **20**
Holme Dr. LN2: Scot .1G **13**
Holme La. NG24: Wint .1G **35**
Holmes, The LN1: Lin .5A **38** (3D **16**)
Holmes Ct. LN5: Nav .4J **31**
Holmes Field LN5: Bass .2D **30**
Holmes La. LN2: Dunh .2E **4**
Holmes Rd. LN1: Lin .4A **38** (3D **16**)
Holmes Way LN8: Wrag .3F **7**
Holmfield LN3: Fis .1K **19** & 3K **19**
Holt, The LN3: Fis .4K **19**
NG24: N'wark T .2A **36**
Holt Cl. LN6: N Hyk .7J **21**
Holyrood Ho. LN2: Lin .5F **11**
Home Cl. LN4: Brace H .3F **23**
Home Ct. LN5: Well .6H **31**
Honeyholes La. LN2: Dunh .4B **4**
Honey Pot Cl. LN2: Lin .6B **12**
Honeys La. NG23: Thpe .7A **36**
Honeysuckle Cl. LN5: Lin .5C **22**
NG24: New B .3G **37**
Honeysuckle La. LN8: Wrag .4G **7**
Honington App. LN1: Lin .6D **10**
Honington Cres. LN1: Lin .6D **10**
Hood St. LN5: Lin .5F **17**
Hoop La. LN8: Lang W .7K **7**
Hope St. LN5: Lin .5F **17**
Horncastle La. LN2: Dunh .4A **4**
Horncastle Rd.
LN8: Wrag, Lang W .4H **7**
Horner Cl. LN5: Lin .5C **22**
Hornsby M. *LN6: Lin .3D 16*
(within The Pavilions Student Village)
Horseshoe Cotts. NG23: Coll .4J **33**
Horse Shoes, The LN4: Meth .4H **29**
Hortonfield Dr. LN4: Wash .4E **18**
Horton Pl. LN1: Sax .3G **9**
Horton St. LN2: Lin .3H **17**
Hospital Cotts. LN4: Brace H .3G **23**
Hotchkin Av. LN1: Sax .3G **9**
Hotel Rd. LN1: Burt W .7J **9**
Hounsfield Cl. NG24: N'wark T .7J **35**
Howard's Gdns. NG24: New B .4G **37**
Howard St. LN1: Lin .2C **16**
Howe Ct. LN2: Lin .7K **11**
Howes Ct. NG24: N'wark T .7E **34**
Huddlestones Wharf NG24: N'wark T .7C **34**
Hudson's La. LN4: H'ton .6G **19**
Hughes Ford Way LN1: Sax .3F **9**
Hughes Ho. LN6: Lin .2B **22**
Hughson Wlk. LN2: Dunh .3E **4**
Hundred Acres La. NG24: Bald .7G **37**
Hungate LN1: Lin .4B **38** (3E **16**)
(not continuous)
Hunters Cl. LN5: Wad .3F **27**
Hunters Dr. LN4: Meth .4H **29**
Hunters Rd. NG24: Bald .5K **37**
Hunt Lea Av. LN6: Lin .6C **16**
Hurn Cl. LN6: Lin .6F **15**
Hurstwood Cl. LN2: Lin .5K **11**
Hutchinson Rd. NG24: N'wark T .7J **35**
Hutson Dr. LN6: N Hyk .5K **21**
Hyde Pk. Cl. LN6: N Hyk .6K **21**
Hykeham Rd. LN6: Lin .4A **22**
Hykeham Sailing Club .6F **21**
Hykeham Station (Rail) .4H **21**

I

Icknield Cl. LN4: Brace H .5G **23**
Industrial Cotts. LN1: Lin .7C **10**
Ingamells Dr. LN1: Sax .3G **9**
Ingham Cl. LN6: Lin .4B **22**
Ingleby Cres. LN2: Lin .5F **11**
Inglewood Cl. NG24: Bald .6H **37**
Innovation Centre, The LN6: Lin .3D **16**
Inns Cl. LN6: N Hyk .4J **21**
Ireton Av. NG24: N'wark T .7J **35**
Iris Cres. LN1: Lin .2C **16**
Ironestone Cl. LN2: Lin .1J **17**
Ivies, The NG24: N'wark T .2A **36**
Ivywood Cl. LN6: Lin .6E **14**

J

Jacobean Rd. LN6: Lin .1H **21**
Jaguar Dr. LN6: N Hyk .6H **21**
Jalland's Row NG24: N'wark T .6E **34**
James Ct. LN2: Welt .1C **4**
James St. LN2: Lin .2C **38** (2F **17**)
James Watt Rd. NG24: N'wark T .4G **35**
Jarvis Cl. LN6: Lin .7K **15**
Jarvis Ho. LN6: Lin .7K **15**
Jasmine Way LN8: Wrag .4G **7**
Jasmin Rd. LN6: Lin .6G **15**
Jason Rd. LN6: Lin .2A **22**
Jellicoe Av. LN2: Lin .2K **17**
Jenison Ho. NG24: N'wark T .4D **36**
Jensen Rd. LN4: Brace H .5F **23**
Jericho Rd. NG24: Bald .6H **37**
Jermyn M. LN4: Wash .5F **19**
Jersey St. NG24: N'wark T .3C **36**
JERUSALEM .3D **14**
Jerusalem LN6: Skel .5D **14**
Jerusalem Cotts. LN6: Skel .4D **14**
Jerusalem Rd. LN6: Skel .3D **14**
Jesmond Vw. LN1: Lin .5E **10**
Jessop Cl. LN3: C Will .1G **19**
NG24: N'wark T .6G **35**
Jessop Way NG24: N'wark T .6G **35**
Jew's House .3C **38** (2F **17**)
John Gold Av. NG24: N'wark T .1F **37**
John Pope Way
NG24: N'wark T .3F **35**
Johns Ct. LN2: Welt .1C **4**
Johnson Dr. LN4: Brace H .3F **23**
Johnsons La. LN6: N Hyk .5J **21**
Johnsons Rd. NG24: Bald .6K **37**
Johnson Vs. LN4: Bran .3E **24**
John St. LN2: Lin .3G **17**
Jolly Jungle Playland .5E **34**
Jubilee Cl. LN3: C Will .7F **13**
LN6: N Hyk .6K **21**
Jubilee Ct. LN2: Nett .1C **12**
Jubilee Dr. LN8: Wrag .4G **7**
Jubilee St. NG24: N'wark T .1E **36**
Julia Rd. LN4: Wash .5F **19**
Julius Way LN6: N Hyk .7G **21**
Juniper Cl. LN4: Bran .3E **24**
LN5: Lin .5C **22**
Juniper Dr. LN2: Scot .7G **5**
Juniper Way LN6: With S .6B **26**
Junxion, The LN5: Lin .6B **38** (4E **16**)

K

Karglen Ind. Est. LN4: Bran .5J **25**
Karsons Way LN2: Welt .1D **4**
Keadby Cl. LN6: Lin .7K **15**
Keats Cl. LN2: Lin .6J **11**
Keats Rd. NG24: Bald .3H **37**
Keddington Av. LN1: Lin .5E **10**
Keeble Dr. LN4: Wash .5F **19**
Keepers Cl. LN2: Welt .1C **4**
Kelham La. NG23: S Mus .2A **34**
NG24: N'wark T .4B **34**
Kelham Rd. NG24: N'wark T .4A **34**
(not continuous)
Kells Cl. LN5: Lin .4D **22**
Kelsey St. LN1: Lin .5B **38** (3E **16**)
Kelstern Cl. LN6: Lin .1G **21**
Kelstern Rd. LN6: Lin .1G **21**
Kemble Cl. LN6: Lin .6F **15**
Kenilworth Cl. LN1: Sax .2E **8**
Kenilworth Dr. LN6: Lin .2C **22**
Kennedy Rd. LN4: Brace H .4F **23**
Kennedy Wlk. NG24: Bald .4J **37**
Kennel La. LN3: Ree .4F **13**
LN6: Dodd .5A **14**
Kennel Wlk. LN3: Ree .5H **13**
Kenner Cl. LN6: Lin .1A **22**
Kenneth St. LN1: Lin .7F **11**
Kennington Cl. LN2: Dunh .4E **4**
Kensington Ho. LN2: Lin .6G **11**
Kent St. LN2: Lin .3J **17**
Kenyon Cl. LN4: H'ton .7F **19**
Kerrison Vw. LN2: Nett .1C **12**
Kershaw Vw. LN1: Lin .5D **10**
Kesteven Ct. LN6: N Hyk .5H **21**
(not continuous)
Kesteven St. LN5: Lin .7C **38** (4F **17**)
(not continuous)
Kestrel Cl. LN6: Lin .6H **15**
Kew Gdns. NG24: New B .4F **37**
Kexby Mill Cl. LN6: N Hyk .7H **21**
Khormaksar Dr. LN4: Noct .6C **28**
Kilburn Cres. LN6: Lin .1A **22**
Kilminster Ct. LN8: Wrag .3G **7**
Kinder Av. LN6: N Hyk .5A **22**
King Dr. LN4: Brace H .5H **23**
Kingfisher Cl. LN6: Lin .6H **15**
NG24: New B .4G **37**
Kings Arms Yd. LN2: Lin .4C **38** (3F **17**)
Kingsdown Rd. LN6: Lin .7F **15**
Kingsley Ct. LN4: Pott .2B **28**
Kingsley Rd. LN6: Lin .2F **21**
Kingsley St. LN1: Lin .1A **38** (1E **16**)
Kingsnorth Cl. NG24: N'wark T .7E **34**
Kings Rd. LN4: Meth .4G **29**
NG24: N'wark T .6D **34**
Kings Sconce Av. NG24: N'wark T .4E **34**
King St. LN5: Lin .7B **38** (4E **16**)
NG24: N'wark T .1C **36**
Kings Way LN2: Welt .1B **4**
Kingsway LN2: Nett .2A **12**
LN5: Lin .5F **17**
NG24: New B .4G **37**
Kinloss Cl. LN6: Lin .1G **21**
Kipling Cl. LN2: Lin .6H **11**
Kirkby St. LN5: Lin .5F **17**
Kirk Ga. NG24: N'wark T .6D **34**
Kirkstall Cl. LN2: Lin .7A **12**
Kirmington Cl. LN6: Lin .1F **21**
Kirton Cl. NG24: Bald .6H **37**
Kneeland LN2: Dunh .3D **4**
Knight Pl. LN5: Lin .6E **16**
Knight's Ct. NG24: N'wark T .7E **34**
Knight St. LN5: Lin .6E **16**
Knight Ter. LN5: Lin .5E **16**
Knipton Cl. NG24: Bald .5H **37**
Knott's Ct. NG24: Bald .4H **37**

L

Laburnum Cl. LN4: Bran .3E **24**
LN6: N Hyk .5K **21**
NG24: New B .3G **37**
Laburnum Ct. LN3: Ree .5J **13**
Laburnum Dr. LN3: C Will .2F **19**
Laceby St. LN2: Lin .3H **17**
Lacey Grn. NG24: Bald .5J **37**
Lacy Cl. LN2: Nett .2D **12**
Ladd's Mill Cl. LN6: N Hyk .7H **21**
Lady Bower Cl. LN6: N Hyk .5A **22**
Lady Elizabeth Ct. LN2: Dunh .3E **4**
Lady Meers Rd. LN3: C Will .7G **13**
LA Fitness
Lincoln, Weaver Rd. .2F **21**
Lincoln, Witham Park Ho. .4G **17**
Newark-on-Trent .5F **35**
Lagonda Cl. LN4: Brace H .5F **23**
Lakeside Cen. NG24: New B .3G **37**
Lake Vw. Cl. LN6: N Hyk .6G **21**
Lake Vw. Rd. LN6: Lin .1C **22**
Lamb Cl. NG24: N'wark T .2A **36**
Lamb Gdns. LN2: Lin .6H **11**
Lancaster Cl. LN5: Wad .3G **27**
(not continuous)
Lancaster Ct. LN2: Welt .2C **4**
Lancaster Pl. LN5: Lin .5F **17**
Lancaster Rd. NG24: Codd .5J **35**
Lancaster Way LN6: Skel .2D **14**
Lancewood Gdns. LN6: Lin .6G **15**
Lancia Cres. LN4: Brace H .5F **23**
Landings, The LN1: Burt W .7J **9**
Landmere Gro. LN6: Lin .5H **15**
Laney Cl. LN2: Lin .6J **11**
Langdale Cl. LN2: Lin .4H **11**
NG24: N'wark T .4C **36**
Langer Cl. LN6: Lin .1F **21**
Langford La. NG23: Holm .3D **32**
Langley Rd. LN6: N Hyk .5H **21**
LANGTON BY WRAGBY .6K **7**
Langton Cl. LN2: Lin .6H **11**
LANGWORTH .5C **6**
Langworthgate LN2: Lin .2E **38** (2G **17**)
Langworth Rd. LN2: Scot .6J **5**
Lannimore Cl. LN5: Lin .4D **22**
Lansbury Rd. NG24: New B .4G **37**
Lansdowne Av. LN6: Lin .2C **22**
Lansdowne Rd. LN5: Nav .4J **31**

A-Z Lincoln 47

Lapwing Cl. LN6: Skel 3E 14
Larch Av. LN2: Nett 2D 12
Larchwood Cres. LN6: Lin 6G 15
Lark Cl. LN8: Wrag 4G 7
Lark Dr. LN5: Well 6J 31
Larkfields NG24: N'wark T 3B 36
Larkin Av. LN3: C Will 1F 19
Larkspur Rd. LN2: Lin 5K 11
Larne Cl. LN5: Lin 5C 22
Larne Rd. LN5: Lin 4D 22
Laughton Cres. LN2: Lin 5G 11
Laughton Way LN2: Lin 5G 11
Laughton Way Nth. LN2: Lin 5F 11
Laureate Ho. LN1: Lin 7F 11
Laurel Cl. LN5: Lin 2D 22
Lavender Cl. LN5: Lin 5C 22
Lavender Dr. LN6: With S 6B 26
Lavender Way NG24: N'wark T 6J 35
Lavenham Gro. LN6: Lin 3A 22
Lawley Cl. LN2: N Gre 5D 12
Lawn, The 2A 38 (2E 16)
Lawn Cotts. LN2: Lin 1B 38 (1E 16)
Lawn Ct. LN1: Lin 1B 38 (1E 16)
Lawns, The NG23: Coll 3J 33
Lawrence Cl. LN6: Lin 7B 16
Lawrence Pl. NG24: N'wark T 6E 34
Lawrence St. NG24: N'wark T 6E 34
Lawson Ct. LN2: Dunh 3F 5
Leach's Bldgs. NG24: N'wark T 1C 36
Learoyd Ho. LN2: Lin 5H 11
Lechler Cl. LN2: Lin 1B 12
Leconfield Cl. LN2: Lin 1G 21
Leconfield Rd. LN6: Lin 7G 15
Lee Av. LN4: H'ton, Wash 6F 19
Leeming Cl. LN6: Lin 1H 21
Lee Rd. LN2: Lin 7G 11
Legbourne Cl. LN1: Lin 6D 10
Le Grand Luce Ct. LN3: C Will 7G 13
Leicester Cl. LN4: Wash 5E 18
Leighton Cres. LN6: Lin 1A 22
Leland Cl. LN2: Lin 7A 12
Lenton Grn. LN2: Lin 6H 11
Lenton Ter. NG24: N'wark T 7C 34
Levellers Way NG24: N'wark T 7J 35
Leveret Chase LN6: With S 6B 26
Lewis St. LN5: Lin 7C 38 (4F 17)
Lexington Ho. LN5: Lin 2D 22
Leyburn Rd. LN6: Lin 3K 21
Ley La. LN5: Bass 5E 30
Leys, The LN3: C Will 7G 13
Ley's Cl. LN6: N Hyk 5H 21
Library Ct. LN1: Sax 3E 8
Lichfield Rd. LN4: Brace H 3G 23
Lievelsley Rd. LN1: Lin 7D 10
Lightfoot Cl. NG24: N'wark T 7J 35
Lilac Cl. LN6: Lin 6G 15
   NG24: N'wark T 4D 36
Lilburne Cl. NG24: N'wark T 7J 35
Lilford Cl. LN2: Lin 6A 12
Lilford Rd. LN2: Lin 6A 12
Lillicrap Ct. LN1: Lin 1B 38 (1E 16)
Lilly's Rd. LN1: Lin 1C 38 (1F 17)
Lily La. NG24: N'wark T 6H 35
Limeberry Pl. LN6: Lin 6E 14
Lime Cres. LN2: N Gre 5D 12
   LN5: Wad 6C 22
Lime Gro. LN3: C Will 1F 19
   LN5: Bass 3D 30
   NG24: N'wark T 1D 36
Lime Kiln Way LN2: Lin 2J 17
Limelands LN2: Lin 2G 17
Lime Tree Av. LN4: Meth 4H 29
Lime Tree Cl. LN6: Lin 6J 15
   NG23: Coll 4H 33
Lime Tree Paddock LN2: Scot 6H 5
LINCOLN 4C 38 (3F 17)
Lincoln Adventure Centre, The 6D 20
Lincoln Arboretum 2G 17
Lincoln Av. LN6: Lin 6C 16
Lincoln Bowl 5J 17
Lincoln Bus. Pk. LN6: Lin 2F 21
Lincoln Castle 2B 38 (2E 16)
Lincoln Cathedral 2D 38 (2F 17)
Lincoln Central Station (Rail) 6C 38 (4F 17)
Lincoln City FC 5F 17
Lincoln Corn Exchange LN5: Lin 5C 38
LINCOLN COUNTY HOSPITAL 2H 17
Lincoln Ct. NG24: N'wark T 4F 35
Lincoln Dr. LN5: Wad 2G 17
   (not continuous)
Lincoln Driving Range 5J 17
Lincoln Golf Cen. 7C 20

Lincoln La. LN6: T Hill 7A 20
Lincoln Lawn Tennis & Bowls Club
   ....1E 38 (1G 17)
Lincoln Relief Rd. LN1: Lin 7A 10
   LN2: Lin 4F 11
   LN6: Lin, Skel, S Hyk 5D 20
Lincoln Rd. LN1: Sax 3G 9
   LN2: Dunh 4D 4
   LN2: Lin, Nett 5J 11
   LN2: Welt, Dunh 2C 4
   LN3: Fis 2H 19
   LN4: Bran, Can 7H 17
   LN4: Duns 2F 29
   LN4: Duns, Noct 7A 28
   LN4: Meth 5G 29
   LN4: Wash 4B 18
   LN5: Bass 3C 30
   LN6: Dodd 6A 14
   LN6: N Hyk 6K 21
   LN6: Skel 2F 15
   NG24: N'wark T 4F 35
Lincoln Rd. Bri. NG24: N'wark T 5E 34
Lincolnshire Archives 4D 38
Lincolnshire Road Transport Mus. ..2H 21
Lincoln St. NG24: N'wark T 5E 34
Lincoln W. Retail Pk. LN6: Lin 5C 16
Linden Av. LN4: Bran 3D 24
   NG24: New B 2F 37
Linden Ct. LN4: Brace H 5G 23
Lindholme Rd. LN6: Lin 1H 21
Lindrick Cl. LN4: H'ton 6F 19
Lindsay Av. NG24: N'wark T 4D 36
Lindum Av. LN2: Lin 3E 38 (2G 17)
Lindum Bus. Pk. LN6: N Hyk 3H 21
Lindum M. LN6: N Hyk 5H 21
   NG24: N'wark T 7E 34
Lindum Rd. LN2: Lin 4D 38 (2F 17)
Lindum Sports Club 1E 38 (1G 17)
Lindum St. NG24: N'wark T 7E 34
Lindum Ter. LN2: Lin 3E 38 (2G 17)
Linga La. LN5: Bass 2D 30
Lingfield Cl. LN1: Sax 1E 8
Link, The LN4: Brace H 3F 23
   LN5: Well 6J 31
Linley Cl. NG23: Coll 4H 33
Linnet Cl. LN6: Lin 6H 15
Linseed Av. NG24: N'wark T 3F 35
Lintin Cl. LN4: H'ton 7F 19
Linton St. LN5: Lin 5F 17
Lisburn Cl. LN5: Lin 5D 22
Lissett Cl. LN6: Lin 1F 21
Lissington Cl. LN2: Lin 6F 11
Lit. Bargate St. LN5: Lin 6E 16
LITTLE CARLTON 1A 34
Lit. Gate La. LN4: Pott 6J 25
Little La. NG23: Coll 5G 33
Lit. Thorpe La. LN6: T Hill 7B 20
Liverpool Dr. LN6: Skel 4F 15
Locking Cl. LN6: Lin 1G 21
Lodge Cl. LN2: Welt 1C 4
   LN6: Lin 2J 21
Lodge Dr. LN4: Bran 4F 25
Lodge La. LN2: Nett 2D 12
Lombard St. NG24: N'wark T 7D 34
Londesborough Way LN4: Meth 5J 29
Londinium Way LN6: N Hyk 7H 21
London Rd. LN4: Brace H 2F 23
   NG24: Bald, New B, N'wark T 7D 34
Longacre Pk. LN6: S Hyk 6E 20
Longdales Pl. LN2: Lin 6G 11
Longdales Rd. LN2: Lin 7F 11
Long Hollow Way NG24: Wint 3H 37
Longfellow Dr. NG24: Bald 3H 37
Longhurst LN6: Lin 6F 15
Longland Wlk. LN2: Lin 6K 11
Long Leys Rd. LN1: Lin 1A 38 (6A 10)
Long Row NG24: N'wark T 7F 35
Longstongs Cres. LN4: Wash 4E 18
Long Wood La. LN4: Blank 7H 29
Lonsdale Cl. LN4: Wash 5D 18
Lonsdale Pl. LN5: Lin 5F 17
Lotus Cl. LN5: Wad 2F 27
Lotus Ct. LN6: N Hyk 6H 21
Louth Rd. LN8: Wrag 3G 7
Loveden Cl. NG24: Bald 5H 37
Loveridge M. NG24: N'wark T 7D 34
Lover's La. NG24: N'wark T 6E 34
Lowfield Cotts. NG24: New B 5E 36
Lowfield La. NG24: Bald, New B 5F 37
Lowfields Cen. LN5: Lin 5D 22

Low Moor Rd. LN6: Lin 2J 2
Low Pk. La. LN4: H'ton 6H 1
Low St. NG23: Coll 5G 3
Lucius Cl. LN6: N Hyk 7F 2
Lucy Tower St. LN1: Lin 5B 38 (3E 1
Ludford Dr. LN6: Lin 7A 1
Lumley Pl. LN5: Lin 5F 1
Lunn La. NG23: Coll 5G 3
Lupin Rd. LN2: Lin 5J 1
Lurgan Cl. LN5: Lin 4D 2
Luton Cl. LN6: Lin 5F 1
Lydd Cl. LN6: Lin 1G 2
Lyndon Bus. Pk. LN6: Lin 2F 2
Lyneham Cl. LN6: Lin 7F 1
Lynmouth Cl. LN6: N Hyk 6A 2
Lysterfield Ct. LN6: N Hyk 6G 2
Lytham Cl. LN4: H'ton 5F 1
Lytton St. LN2: Lin 3G 1

M

Macaulay Cl. NG24: Bald 3H 3
Macaulay Dr. LN2: Lin 7H 1
   NG24: Bald 3H 3
McInnes St. LN2: Lin 3J 1
Mackleys La. NG23: N Mus 4C 3
Macmillan Av. LN6: N Hyk 6G 2
Macphail Cres. LN1: Sax 3G
Madden Cl. LN5: Lin 7C 1
Magdalene Vw. NG24: N'wark T 7F 3
Magistrates' Court
   Lincoln 7B 38 (4E 1
Magnolia Cl. LN4: Bran 3D 2
Magnus Ct. LN6: N Hyk 7G 2
Magnus St. NG24: N'wark T 6E 3
Magpie Cl. LN6: Skel 3E 1
Magpie Sq. LN2: Lin 5D 3
Maiden Cl. LN1: Sax 3F
Maidenwell Cl. LN5: Nav 4J 3
Maidenwell La. LN5: Nav 4H 3
Maidment Dr. LN1: Lin 6C 1
Main Av. LN4: Brace H 4F 2
Main Dr. LN2: Scot 1J 1
Main Rd. LN3: L'worth 4C
   LN4: Noct 6B 2
   LN4: Pott 2A 2
   LN4: Wash 4D 1
Main St. LN1: Burt L 3B 1
   LN2: Scot 7G
   LN4: Noct 6B 2
   LN5: Booth G 1H 3
   LN6: Dodd 5A 1
   LN6: T Hill 7B 2
   NG23: N Mus 3C 3
   NG23: S Mus 1B 3
   NG24: Bald 4H 3
Mainwaring Cl. LN2: Dunh 3E
Mainwaring Rd. LN2: Lin 1E 38 (1G 1
Malham Cl. LN6: Lin 5G 1
Malham Dr. LN6: Lin 4G 1
Mallard Cl. LN6: Lin 5J 1
   LN6: Skel 3E 1
Mallard Ct. LN6: N Hyk 6G 2
Mallard Grn. NG24: New B 3G 3
Mallory Cl. LN6: Lin 7G 1
Mall Shop Centre, The
   LN2: Lin 4C 38 (3F 1
Malt Kiln Cotts. LN8: Wrag 3F
Malt Kiln La. LN5: Wad 4E 2
Maltkiln La. NG24: N'wark T 5E 3
Malton Rd. LN4: N'wark T 4K 3
Maltsters, The NG24: N'wark T 2A 3
Malus Cl. LN4: Bran 3D 2
Malvern Av. LN4: Wash 5F
Malvern Cl. LN5: Lin 3D 2
   LN6: N Hyk 7J 2
Manby St. LN5: Lin 1D 2
Manchester Rd. LN5: Wad 3G 1
Manners Rd. NG24: Bald 5G
   NG24: N'wark T 6C
Manor Cl. LN2: Lin 1F
   LN4: Meth 5J
Manor Ct. LN2: Nett 2A 1
   LN2: Scot 1G
   LN2: Welt 2C
   LN4: Noct 5B
   LN5: Carl M 7C
Manor Dr. LN2: Scot 1G
   LN8: Wrag 4H
Manor Grounds LN6: Skel 2F
Manor Ho. Dr. NG23: N Mus 3O

Manor La. LN1: Bro 5E 8
  LN2: Welt .2C 4
  LN4: Meth 5J 29
  LN5: Carl M 7C 30
  LN5: Wad 3E 26
Manor Leas Cl. LN6: Lin 4B 22
Manor Orchard LN5: Bass 4C 30
Manor Paddocks LN5: Bass 4C 30
Manor Ri. LN3: Ree 5H 13
Manor Rd. LN1: Sax 2E 8
  LN2: Lin .1G 17
  LN4: Wash 5D 18
  LN6: N Hyk 6J 21
  NG23: Coll 4H 33
Manor Way LN2: Dunh 3E 4
Manrico Dr. LN1: Lin 6C 10
Manse Av. LN5: Lin 3D 22
Mansford Cl. LN2: Nett 1B 12
Manthorpe Ho. NG24: Bald 4J 37
Manthorpe Way NG24: Bald 4J 37
Manton Rd. LN2: Lin 6F 11
Manvers Ct. LN2: Lin 3J 17
Maple Cl. LN4: Brace H 5H 23
  LN5: Wad 7C 22
Maple Ct. LN1: Sax 2D 8
Maple Dr. LN2: Scot 1H 13
  LN5: Bass 2E 30
Maple Gro. NG24: N'wark T 4D 36
Maple Leaf Ct. NG24: N'wark T 4F 35
Maple St. LN5: Lin 2D 22
Mappleton LN6: N Hyk 7G 21
Marcus Cl. LN6: N Hyk 7F 21
Mareham Cl. LN4: Brace H 5G 23
Marham Cl. LN6: Lin 6F 15
Marigold Cl. LN2: Lin 5J 11
Marina Cl. LN5: Wad 4F 27
               (Millers Rd.)
  LN5: Wad 2F 27
             (Vanwall Dr.)
Marine App. LN1: Burt W 7J 9
Marine Point Apartments LN1: Burt W . .7J 9
Marine Wlk. LN1: Burt W 7J 9
Marjorie Av. LN6: Lin 6D 16
Market Pl. LN8: Wrag 4G 7
  NG24: N'wark T 7D 34
Market Rasen Rd. LN2: Dunh 3E 4
Markham Av. NG24: N'wark T 4F 35
Markwick Cl. NG24: N'wark T 7H 35
Marlborough Av. LN4: Wash 5E 18
Marlborough Cl. LN2: Lin 5J 11
  NG24: N'wark T 3B 36
Marlborough Ct. LN4: Wash 5D 18
  NG24: N'wark T 3B 36
Marlborough Ho. LN2: Lin 6H 11
Marles Cl. NG24: N'wark T 5G 35
Marlowe Dr. LN2: Lin 7H 11
  NG24: Bald 4J 37
Marne Gdns. LN1: Lin 7E 10
Marquis Av. NG24: Bald 5H 37
Marrat Cl. LN2: Lin 7K 11
Marriner Ct. LN2: Lin 7G 11
Marriner Cres. LN2: Lin 7G 11
Marron Cl. NG24: Bald 6K 37
Marshall Ct. NG24: Bald 4J 37
Marsh La. NG23: N Mus 4C 32
Marston Cl. NG24: Bald 5G 37
Marston Moor Rd. NG24: N'wark T . . .7J 35
Martin Cl. LN4: H'ton 7F 19
  LN6: Skel 3E 14
Martin St. LN5: Lin 5F 17
Marton Rd. NG24: N'wark T 2F 37
Mary Sookias Ho. LN1: Lin 1C 38 (1F 17)
Masefield Cres. NG24: Bald 4H 37
Massey Cl. NG24: N'wark T 7F 35
Massey Rd. LN2: Lin 1G 17
Massey St. NG24: N'wark T 7F 35
Mather Rd. NG24: N'wark T 6D 34
Matilda Rd. LN6: Lin 5D 16
Matlock Dr. LN6: N Hyk 5J 21
Maun Grn. NG24: N'wark T 5F 35
Maximus Rd. LN6: N Hyk 7F 21
Maxwell Av. LN6: Lin 6C 16
Mayall Ct. LN5: Wad 3F 27
Mayall Wlk. LN5: Wad 3F 27
May Cres. LN1: Lin 3H 11
Mayfair Av. LN6: Lin 2D 16
Mayfair Cl. LN3: C Will 6G 13
Mays La. LN5: Lin 3F 9
Maythorne Cl. NG24: New B 3G 37
Mead, The LN6: Lin 2A 22
Mead Cl. LN6: Lin 2A 22
Meadow Bank Av. LN3: Fis 3K 19

Meadow Cl. LN2: Scot 6H 5
  LN3: Ree 5J 13
  LN4: Meth 4J 29
  LN6: N Hyk 7K 21
  NG23: N Mus 5C 32
Meadow Farm Caravan Site
  LN6: N Hyk 7K 21
Meadowlake Cl. LN6: Lin 5J 15
Meadowlake Cres. LN6: Lin 5H 15
Meadow La. LN5: Wad 1A 26
  LN6: N Hyk . . . . .7K 21 & 1A 26
  LN6: S Hyk 3A 26
Meadow Rise LN1: Sax 2F 9
Meadow Rd. LN4: Duns 2H 29
  NG24: New B 4G 37
Meadows La. LN3: Ree 4J 13
Meadow Way LN2: Welt 2D 4
  LN4: Brace H 5G 23
Mead Way NG24: Bald 5F 37
Meadway LN3: C Will 7G 13
Medieval Bishop's Palace, The 3D 38
Medway Cres. LN6: N Hyk 5B 22
Meering Av. NG24: N'wark T 3F 35
Meering Cl. NG23: Coll 3H 33
Megs La. LN5: Nav 5J 31
Melbourne Cl. LN1: Lin 7G 15
Melbourne Rd. LN6: Lin 6G 15
Melbourne Way LN5: Wad 1C 26
Meldrum Cres. NG24: N'wark T 3C 36
Mellows Cl. LN3: Ree 5H 13
Melrose La. LN6: Lin 6F 15
Melville Cl. LN4: Bran 4E 24
Melville St. LN5: Lin 5D 38 (3F 17)
Memorial Hall Dr. LN5: Well 6H 31
Mendip Av. LN6: N Hyk 7J 21
Mendip Cl. LN5: Lin 4D 22
Mercer Dr. LN1: Lin 7D 10
Mercia Rd. NG24: N'wark T 3D 36
Mercury Cl. LN6: N Hyk 6G 21
Mere Rd. LN4: Brace H, Bran 7D 24
  LN5: Wad 3F 27
Merleswen LN2: Dunh 3D 4
Merrycock La. LN4: H'ton 7F 19
METHERINGHAM 5H 29
Metheringham Cl. LN6: Lin 7H 15
Metheringham Fen La. LN4: Meth 4J 29
Metheringham Heath La. LN4: Meth . . .5F 29
Metheringham Station (Rail) 5K 29
Meynell Av. LN6: Lin 6C 16
Meyrick Rd. NG24: N'wark T 6E 34
Michaelgate LN1: Lin 3C 38 (2F 17)
Middlebrook Cl. LN6: Lin 2A 22
Middlebrook Rd. LN6: Lin 2K 21
Middle Ga. NG24: N'wark T 7D 34
Middlegate LN5: Bass 3D 30
Middle La. LN6: T Hill 7C 20
Middle St. LN1: S Car, Burt L 1B 10
  LN4: Duns 2G 29
  LN4: Meth 5H 29
  LN4: Pott 2A 28
  LN6: N Hyk 7K 21
Middleton Rd. NG24: N'wark T 4F 35
Middleton's Fld. LN2: Lin 1D 38 (1F 17)
Middleway LN3: C Will 1G 19
Midholm LN3: C Will 1G 19
Midia Cl. LN1: Lin 6C 10
Midland Ter. NG24: N'wark T 6C 34
Midville Cl. LN1: Lin 5E 10
Midway Cl. LN2: Nett 1C 12
Mildenhall Dr. LN6: Lin 6F 15
Mildmay St. LN1: Lin 7E 10
Milfoil Av. LN1: Lin 2C 16
Millbeck Dr. LN2: Lin 4G 11
Millbrook Cl. LN6: N Hyk 7H 21
Millbrook La. LN8: Wrag 4F 7
Mill Ct. LN1: Lin 1E 16
Millers Cl. LN4: H'ton 6E 18
Millers Dale LN6: N Hyk 5K 21
Millers Rd. LN5: Wad 4F 27
Millfield Av. LN1: Sax 2F 9
Millfield Rd. LN4: Meth 5G 29
Mill Ga. NG24: N'wark T 1C 36
Millgate LN5: Well 6H 31
Millgate Mus. 7C 34
Mill Grn. NG24: N'wark T 7F 35
Mill Hill LN2: Nett 2B 12
Mill Ho. LN1: Lin 4A 38 (3E 16)
Mill La. LN1: Sax 2F 9
  LN4: H'ton 6F 19
  LN5: Lin .5E 16
  LN6: N Hyk 7H 21

Mill La. NG23: N Mus, S Mus 5B 32
             (not continuous)
  NG24: N'wark T 7C 34
Mill Mere Rd. LN5: Wad 2F 27
Mill Moor Way LN6: N Hyk 6H 21
Mill Ri. LN2: Scot 7H 5
  LN5: Well 6H 31
Mill Rd. LN1: Lin 1A 38 (1E 16)
Mill Row LN1: Lin 1E 16
Mills Dr. NG24: N'wark T 2A 36
Mill Stone La. LN5: Wad 2F 27
Millstream Rd. LN4: H'ton 6F 19
Mill Vw. Ct. LN8: Wrag 4G 7
Mill Vw. Rd. LN8: Wrag 4G 7
Milman Rd. LN2: Lin 3H 17
Milner St. NG24: N'wark T 1E 36
Milton Cl. LN3: C Will 1G 19
  LN4: Bran 3C 24
Milton St. LN1: Lin 1E 22
  NG24: New B 2F 37
Minerva Way LN6: N Hyk 6G 21
Minster Cl. LN4: Brace H 3G 23
Minster Dr. LN3: C Will 6G 13
Minster Yd. LN2: Lin 2C 38 (2F 17)
             (not continuous)
Minting Cl. LN1: Lin 4B 38 (3E 16)
Mint St. LN1: Lin 4B 38 (3E 16)
Mitchell Cl. LN6: Skel 2E 14
Mitchell Dr. LN1: Lin 7C 10
Monce Cl. LN2: Welt 1B 4
Monckton Way LN2: Dunh 4D 4
Monks Leys Ter. LN2: Lin 2G 17
Monks Mnr. Ct. LN2: Lin 1H 17
Monks Mnr. Dr. LN2: Lin 2H 17
Monks Rd. LN2: Lin 4D 38 (3F 17)
Monks Way LN2: Lin 3K 17
Monkwood Cl. NG23: Coll 3J 33
Monsal Dale LN6: N Hyk 5K 21
Monson Cl. LN5: Lin 7B 38 (5E 16)
Monson M. LN5: Lin 7B 38
Monson Pk. LN6: Skel 2E 14
Monson St. LN5: Lin 7B 38 (5E 16)
Mons Pl. LN1: Lin 7E 10
Montague St. LN2: Lin 4E 38 (3G 17)
Montague Ter. LN2: Lin 4E 38 (3G 17)
Montagu Rd. LN4: Can 6H 17
Montaigne Cl. LN2: Lin 6K 11
Montaigne Cres. LN2: Lin 6K 11
Montaigne Gdn. LN2: Lin 6K 11
Montgomery Rd. NG24: N'wark T 3E 36
Montrose Cl. LN6: N Hyk 6J 21
Moorby Cl. LN1: Lin 6E 10
Moorhen Cl. LN6: With S 7A 26
Moorhouse La. NG23: S Mus 5A 32
Moorings, The LN1: Burt W 7J 9
Moorland Av. LN6: Lin 2A 22
Moorland Cen. LN6: N Hyk 2K 21
Moorland Cl. LN5: Carl M 7C 30
  LN6: Lin .2K 21
Moorland Cres. LN6: Lin 1B 22
Moorlands, The LN4: Meth 5K 29
Moorland Way LN6: Lin 2K 21
Moor La. LN3: Ree 4J 13
             (not continuous)
  LN4: Bran 4F 25
  LN4: Meth 5K 29
  LN4: Pott 2A 28
  LN5: Thurl 7A 26
  LN6: N Hyk 6H 21
  LN6: T Hill 7A 26
  LN6: With S 7A 26
Moor Rd. NG23: Coll 3J 33
MOORS, THE 2J 25
Moorside Ct. LN6: N Hyk 7J 21
Moor St. LN1: Lin 2D 16
Morden Cl. LN4: Meth 5J 29
Morris Cl. LN2: Dunh 3E 4
Morton Dr. LN6: Lin 7K 15
Motherby Hill LN1: Lin 3B 38 (2E 16)
Motherby La. LN1: Lin 3B 38 (2E 16)
Moulton Cres. NG24: New B 5G 37
Mount, The NG24: N'wark T 6D 34
Mount Ct. NG24: Bald 4G 37
Mount St. LN1: Lin 7E 10
  NG24: N'wark T 6D 34
             (off Mount La.)
Mount La. NG24: N'wark T 7E 34
Mountney Pl. NG24: N'wark T 4F 35
Mount Rd. LN4: Brace H 4F 23
  NG24: Bald 4G 37
Mount St. LN1: Lin 7E 10
Mourn Ter. LN5: Lin 5D 22

Moxons La. LN5: Wad 3F 27
Mrs Smith's Cottage Mus. 4J 31
Much La. LN1: Lin 5B 38 (3E 16)
Muirfield Cl. LN6: Lin 7F 15
Mulberry Av. LN6: N Hyk 5K 21
Mulberry Cl. LN5: Wad 6C 22
Mumby Cl. NG24: N'wark T 6E 34
Muntjac Way LN6: With S 6A 26
Murdock Rd. LN5: Lin 1D 22
Murfin Ho. LN6: Lin 2B 22
Museum Cl. LN2: Lin 4C 38
Museum of Lincolnshire Life 1A 38 (1E 16)
Musgraves Orchard LN2: Welt 1E 4
Muskham La. NG23: Bath 4A 32
Muskham Vw. NG24: N'wark T 6D 34

N

Naam Gro. LN1: Lin 1B 38 (1E 16)
Naam Pl. LN1: Lin 1B 38 (1E 16)
Napier St. LN2: Lin 3H 17
Narrow Moor La. LN5: Bass 1E 30
                                         (not continuous)
Naseby Av. NG24: N'wark T 7J 35
Nash La. LN6: N Hyk 6J 21
Natal Vw. LN1: Lin 5D 10
Natural World Cen. 6B 20
NAVENBY 4J 31
Navenby Bowls Club 5J 31
Navenby La. LN5: Bass 5C 30
Navigation Yd. NG24: N'wark T 7C 34
Neale Ct. LN6: N Hyk 7J 21
Neale Rd. LN6: N Hyk 7J 21
Neile Cl. LN2: Lin 6K 11
Nelson Dr. LN4: Wash 4D 18
Nelson La. NG23: N Mus 4B 32
Nelson Rd. LN3: Fis . . . . .2K 19 & 4K 19
  NG24: New B 4F 37
Nelson St. LN1: Lin 3D 16
Nelthorpe St. LN5: Lin 7B 38 (5E 16)
Nene Pk. LN6: N Hyk 6G 21
Nene Rd. LN1: Lin 5E 10
Nero Way LN6: N Hyk 7F 21
NETTLEHAM .2B 12
Nettleham Cl. LN2: Lin 7G 11
Nettleham M. LN2: Lin 5H 11
Nettleham Rd. LN2: Lin 1D 38 (1F 17)
  LN2: Nett, Scot 7E 4
Nettleham Rd. Shop. Cen. LN2: Lin 5J 11
Nettleham Vw. LN2: Lin 5H 11
Nettleton Cl. LN4: Bran 3E 24
Nettleton Dr. LN6: With S 5C 26
Nettleton Ho. LN2: Lin 5H 11
Neustadt Ct. LN2: Lin 3C 38 (2F 17)
Nevile Wlk. LN5: Well 6H 31
Newark Air Mus. 2K 35
Newark & Notts Gliding Club 2K 35
Newark Bus. Pk. NG24: N'wark T 6F 35
Newark Castle 6D 34
Newark Castle Station (Rail) 6D 34
Newark Golf Centre (Driving Range) 2J 35
NEWARK HOSPITAL 2E 36
Newark Northgate Station (Rail) 5F 35
NEWARK-ON-TRENT 7D 34
Newark Rd. LN5: Bass 3C 30
  LN5: Lin 3A 22
  LN6: N Hyk, S Hyk 7E 20
  NG23: Coll .6G 33
  NG24: Codd 6J 35
  NG24: Hawt 5B 36
Newark Showground 2K 35
Newark Visitors Cen. 1C 36
NEW BALDERTON 3G 37
NEWBALL 4E 6
NEW BOULTHAM 6A 38 (3D 16)
Newbury Rd. NG24: N'wark T 6J 35
Newcastle Av. NG24: N'wark T 2E 36
Newcot La. LN4: H'ton 7H 19
New Cres. LN3: C Will 7F 13
Newhaven Dr. LN5: Lin 4D 22
Newland LN1: Lin 4A 38 (3E 16)
Newland St. W. LN1: Lin 3A 38 (2D 16)
Newnham Rd. NG24: N'wark T 6E 34
Newport LN1: Lin 1C 38
Newport Arch .1C 38
Newport Ct. LN1: Lin 1C 38 (1F 17)
Newport Cres. LN5: Wad 2F 27
Newporte Bus. Pk. LN1: Lin 1J 17
Newstead Av. LN3: C Will 1G 19
  NG24: N'wark T 6E 34
New St. NG24: N'wark T 7E 34

Newsums Vs. LN1: Lin 2C 16
New Swan Cl. LN6: With S 7A 26
New Ten Row LN4: Noct 6B 28
Newton Cl. LN4: Meth 4H 29
  LN8: Wrag .4H 7
Newton Dr. LN3: C Will 7D 12
Newton St. LN5: Lin 5D 38 (3F 17)
  NG24: N'wark T 1F 37
NHS WALK-IN CENTRE (LINCOLN)
  . . . . .4E 38 (3G 17)
Nicholson Ct. NG24: N'wark T 1E 36
Nicholson St. NG24: N'wark T 1E 36
Nicholson's Wharf
  NG24: N'wark T 6D 34
Nightingale Cl. NG24: Bald 4J 37
Nightingale Cres. LN6: Lin 6H 15
Nixon Way NG23: Coll 3H 33
Noble Ho. NG24: N'wark T 4D 36
NOCTON 6B 28
Nocton Dr. LN2: Lin 5F 11
Nocton Fen La. LN4: Noct 4B 28
Nocton Pk. Rd. LN4: Noct 5B 28
Nocton Rd. LN4: Noct, Pott 3B 28
Norbeck La. LN2: Welt 2B 4
Norfolk Cres. LN4: Brace H 3F 23
Norfolk St. LN1: Lin 2D 16
Norman Av. NG24: N'wark T 3F 35
Norman Cres. LN4: Meth 5G 29
Norman St. LN5: Lin 6C 38 (4F 17)
Normanton Rd. NG24: N'wark T 6H 35
Norris St. LN5: Lin 5F 17
North Ct. LN2: Nett 1B 12
Northcroft LN1: Sax 1E 8
Northcroft La. NG23: Coll 2F 33
Nth. Dales Rd. LN4: Wash . . . .4J 19 & 4K 19
North Dr. NG24: Bald 6J 37
Northern Rd. NG24: N'wark T 5F 35
Northfield Av. LN2: Scot 1H 13
Northfield Ri. LN1: Sax 2D 8
Northfield Rd. LN2: Welt 1D 4
North Gate NG24: N'wark T 6D 34
                                         (not continuous)
Northgate LN2: Lin 1D 38 (1F 17)
Northgate Retail Pk. NG24: N'wark T 5E 34
NORTH GREETWELL 5C 12
NORTH HYKEHAM 5H 21
Northing La. LN2: Scot 5H 5
North Kesteven Sports Cen. 6H 21
North La. LN3: Ree 4G 13
  LN5: Nav 4J 31
NORTH MUSKHAM 4C 32
Northorpe Cl. LN6: Lin 7K 15
North Pde. LN1: Lin 3A 38 (2E 16)
North St. LN2: Nett 1B 12
North Way LN6: N Hyk 5H 21
Norton Disney Rd. LN5: Carl M 4A 30
Norton La. LN6: With S 7A 26
Norwich Cl. LN4: Wash 5G 19
Norwich Dr. LN4: Brace H 4G 23
Nottingham Ter. LN2: Lin 3E 38 (2G 17)
Novona Ho. LN2: Lin 7K 11
Nursery Cl. LN1: Sax 2E 8
  LN2: Dunh .3F 5
  LN3: L'worth 5B 6
Nursery Ct. NG24: N'wark T 6E 34
Nursery Gdns. NG24: Bald 5H 37
Nursery Gro. LN2: Lin 7G 11
Nurses La. LN6: Skel 1E 14

O

Oak Av. LN2: Dunh 3E 4
Oak Cl. LN2: Scot 1H 13
Oak Ct. LN6: Lin 3A 22
Oak Cres. LN3: C Will 1F 19
Oakdene Av. LN4: Brace H 5G 23
Oak Dr. NG24: New B 3G 37
Oak Farm Paddock LN6: N Hyk 6G 21
Oakfield LN1: Sax 2E 8
Oakfield Rd. NG24: Bald 7K 37
Oakfield St. LN2: Lin 3H 17
Oak Hill LN4: Wash 4D 18
Oakland Cl. LN1: Lin 6D 10
Oaklands LN1: Sax 2E 8
  LN4: Bran .4E 24
  NG23: Coll .4H 33
Oaklands, The LN8: Wrag 4H 7
Oaklands Cl. NG23: Coll 5H 33
Oakleigh Dr. LN1: Lin 7C 10
Oakleigh Ter. LN1: Lin 7C 10

Oaks, The LN2: Nett 2D 12
  LN2: Scot 7G 5
  NG24: New B 4G 37
Oak Tree Dr. LN6: With S 7A 26
Oak Vw. LN2: Dunh 3E 4
  NG24: N'wark T 7G 35
Oakview LN6: Lin 5H 15
Oakwood Av. LN6: Lin 6G 15
Oakwood Cl. LN3: C Will 1G 19
Oakwood Rd. LN6: Lin 1F 21
Oberon Cl. LN1: Lin 7C 10
Occupation La. LN1: Bro 6E 8
  LN2: Welt 2C 4
Occupation Rd. LN1: Lin 1B 38 (1E 16)
Octavian Cres. LN6: N Hyk 7F 21
ODDER 4J 9
Odeon Cinema
  Lincoln 5B 38
Old Brick Kiln La. LN5: Bass 4D 30
Old Brickyard, The LN5: Lin 4D 22
Old Chapel Rd. LN6: Skel 2E 14
Old Cobham Orchard NG24: New B 3F 37
Old Fellows Cl. LN3: L'worth 5B 6
Old Grammar School Way
  LN8: Wrag .3G 7
Old Great Nth. Rd. NG23: N Mus 3B 32
Old Hall Gdns. NG24: Codd 6K 35
Old Mill, The LN5: Lin 5D 16
Old Mill Cres. NG24: N'wark T 7F 35
Old Oak Ri. LN6: Skel 2F 15
Old Palace, The LN2: Lin 3D 38
Old Pitts Cl. LN6: Skel 3D 14
Old Pond Cl. LN6: Lin 6H 15
Old Rectory Ct. NG24: Wint 1G 35
Old School La.
  NG24: N'wark T 1F 37
Old School Yd. LN2: Welt 2C 4
                                         (off Cliff Rd.)
Old Stack Yard, The LN4: H'ton 6G 19
Old Ten Row LN4: Noct 6B 28
Old Vicarage Gdns.
  LN6: Nett 3F 15
Old Wood LN6: Skel 1B 14
Old Wood Cl. LN6: Lin 5G 15
Oliver Cl. NG24: N'wark T 7F 35
Olive St. LN1: Lin 7E 10
Ollerton Rd. NG23: Lit C . . . . . . .1A 34 & 7A 32
Olsen Ct. LN2: Lin 7K 11
Olsen Ri. LN2: Lin 7K 11
Orchard, The LN4: Wash 4C 18
  NG24: N'wark T 2F 37
Orchard Cl. LN2: Scot 7H 5
  LN2: Welt 2D 4
  LN3: C Will .1F 19
  LN4: Duns .1H 29
  LN4: Meth .5H 29
  LN5: Bass .2D 30
  LN6: Lin 7F 15
  NG23: S Mus 7B 32
Orchard Gth. LN5: Wad 1D 26
Orchard La. LN1: Sax 2E 8
Orchard Pk. NG24: Codd 5K 35
Orchard Rd. LN3: Fis 1K 19
Orchard St. LN1: Lin 4A 38 (3E 16)
Orchard Wlk. LN5: Brace H 1E 22
Orchard Way LN2: Nett 1C 12
  NG24: Bald .5H 37
Orchid Cl. NG24: New B 3F 37
Orchid Rd. LN5: Lin 5C 22
Ordoyno Gro. NG24: Codd 5K 35
Orston Av. NG24: N'wark T 2C 36
Osborne Cl. LN1: Lin 7E 10
Osiers, The NG24: N'wark T 2A 36
Ossington M. NG24: N'wark T 6D 34
                                         (off Bar Gate)
Ossington Way NG24: N'wark T 6D 34
Otter Av. LN1: Sax 2E 8
Otter Bank NG24: N'wark T 5E 34
Otters Cotts. LN5: Lin 7D 16
Oulton Cl. LN6: N Hyk 5A 22
Oundle Cl. LN4: Wash 5E 18
Outer Circ. Dr. LN2: Lin 6H 11
Outer Circ. Grn. LN2: Lin 7J 11
Outer Circ. Rd. LN2: Lin 7K 11
Oval, The LN2: Lin 6H 11
Oval App. LN2: Lin 6H 11
                                         (not continuous)
Overton Cl. LN5: Nav 4J 31
Owl Cl. LN6: With S 6A 26
Owls End LN2: Welt 1E 4
Oxeney Dr. LN3: L'worth 5C 6
Oxen Pk. Cl. LN2: Lin 4G 11

Oxford Cl. LN4: Wash 5E 18
Oxford St. LN5: Lin 6C 38 (4F 17)

P

Pach Way NG24: Bald 6K 37
Paddock, The LN2: Scot 2H 13
  LN3: C Will 7G 13
  LN4: Can 6H 17
  LN6: Skel 2E 14
  NG23: Coll 5H 33
Paddock Cl. LN4: Brace H 5G 23
Paddock La. LN4: Bran 4E 24
  LN4: Meth 4H 29
Paddocks, The LN4: Pott 1A 28
  NG24: N'wark T 1F 37
Padley Rd. LN2: Lin 7K 11
Painshall Cl. LN2: Welt 1C 4
Palace Theatre
  Newark-on-Trent 7E 34
Palatine Ho. LN2: Lin 7K 11
Palmer Rd. LN2: Lin 7G 11
Palmer St. LN5: Lin 7D 38 (5F 17)
Parade, The LN3: C Will 7G 13
Paradise Row LN6: Dodd 6A 14
Park, The LN1: Lin 4B 38 (3E 16)
  LN4: Pott 3A 28
  NG23: N Mus 3C 32
  NG24: N'wark T 2E 36
Park Av. LN4: Wash 4E 18
  LN6: Lin 6K 15
Park Cl. LN2: Scot 1H 13
Park Ct. LN1: Lin 4B 38 (3E 16)
Park Cres. LN4: Meth 5K 29
  LN4: Wash 5E 18
  NG24: N'wark T 4F 35
Parker Av. LN5: Lin 3D 22
Parker Cres. LN5: Lin 3D 22
Parker St. NG24: N'wark T 7E 34
Park Hill LN3: C Will 1G 19
Parklands LN5: Wad 3G 27
Parklands Av. LN4: Noct 5B 28
Parklands Cl. NG24: Codd 5K 35
Parkland Way LN8: Wrag 4F 7
Park La. LN1: Burt W 6J 9
  LN4: Brace H 3G 23
  LN4: H'ton 6G 19
  LN4: Wash 5E 18
  LN5: 1D 22
Parksgate Av. LN6: Lin 2K 21
Parkside LN2: Nett 4C 12
Park St. LN1: Lin 4B 38 (3E 16)
Park Vw. Av. LN4: Bran 3C 24
Parkview Ct. LN4: Brace H 4F 23
Park Vw. M. LN4: Bran 3C 24
Parkway NG24: N'wark T 2C 36
Parliament Ct. NG24: N'wark T 7C 34
Parliament St. NG24: N'wark T 7C 34
Parliament Wlk. NG24: N'wark T 1C 36
  (off Parliament St.)
Parsons Cl. NG24: Bald 6J 37
Partridge Grn. LN6: With S 6A 26
Pastures, The LN2: Welt 2D 4
Patch Rd. LN6: With S 7B 26
Pateley Moor Ct. LN6: N Hyk 7J 21
Pavilion, The LN1: Lin 6D 10
Pavilions Student Village, The LN6: Lin 3D 16
Pavillion Gdns. LN6: Lin 3A 22
Paving Way LN6: Lin 3G 21
Paxtons Ct. NG24: N'wark T 6D 34
Paynell LN2: Dunh 3D 4
Peak Dale LN6: N Hyk 5J 21
Pear Tree Cl. LN6: Lin 5G 15
Peddars Ct. LN4: Brace H 5G 23
Peebles Rd. NG24: N'wark T 3B 36
Peel St. LN5: Lin 5E 16
Peets Dr. NG23: N Mus 4C 32
Pelham Bri. LN5: Lin 6D 38 (4F 17)
Pelham Cl. LN2: Scot 1H 13
  NG24: N'wark T 7C 34
Pelham Gdns. NG24: N'wark T 7D 34
Pelham La. LN4: Can 6H 17
Pelham St. LN5: Lin 6D 38 (4F 17)
  NG24: N'wark T 7C 34
Pembertons Pl. LN3: Ree 4H 13
Pembrey Cl. LN6: Lin 7G 15
Pembroke Cres. NG24: N'wark T 4G 35
Pendennis LN5: Lin 1E 22
Pendine Cres. LN6: N Hyk 6A 22
Pendred Av. LN6: With S 7B 26

Penfold La. LN4: Wash 4E 18
Pennell St. LN5: Lin 5E 16
Pennycress Cl. LN2: Lin 5J 11
Penrose Cl. LN6: N Hyk 7J 21
Penswick Gro. NG24: Codd 5K 35
Pentland Dr. LN6: N Hyk 7J 21
Peppercorn Cl. LN6: Lin 5D 16
Percy St. LN2: Lin 3H 17
Peregrine M. LN3: Lin 2A 18
Perney Cres. LN6: N Hyk 7J 21
Perry Ct. LN4: Brace H 3F 23
Pershore Way LN6: Lin 1G 21
Peterborough Rd. NG23: Coll 3H 33
Peter Hodgkinson Cen. LN2: Lin 2J 17
Petersfield Cl. LN6: Lin 7F 15
Philip Cl. LN6: N Hyk 6K 21
Philip Rd. NG24: N'wark T 3C 36
Phillipott Cl. NG24: N'wark T 7H 35
Phillips Ct. LN2: Welt 1C 4
Phoenix La. NG24: Bald 6K 37
Photinia Cl. LN4: Bran 3E 24
Picton St. LN6: Lin 3D 16
Pierson St. NG24: N'wark T 3C 36
Pietermaritz St. LN1: Lin 5E 10
Pietermaritz Vw. LN1: Lin 5E 10
Pigot Way LN1: Lin 7K 11
Pine Cl. LN1: Lin 5F 11
  LN5: Wad 7C 22
  NG24: Bald 7K 37
  NG24: N'wark T 3F 35
Pinewood Cres. LN6: Lin 6F 15
Pinfold Cl. LN5: Bass 2D 30
  NG23: Coll 3H 33
Pinfold La. NG24: Bald 5H 37
Pingle La. LN5: Well 7J 31
Pioneer Way LN6: Lin 3J 21
Pippin Ct. NG24: N'wark T 5F 35
Pitcairn Av. LN2: Lin 7K 11
Pitts Rd. LN4: Wash 5E 18
Platts, The NG24: N'wark T 2C 36
Pleasant Ter. LN5: Lin 6E 16
  (off Craven St.)
Plough La. LN3: Fis 1K 19
  LN3: Ree 5H 13
Ploughmans Ct. LN2: Lin 7A 12
Ploughmans La. LN2: Lin 7A 12
Ploughmans Wlk. LN2: Lin 7A 12
  (off Ploughmans Ct.)
Plover Gro. LN6: Lin 6J 15
Plum Way NG24: Bald 6J 37
Poachers Brook LN6: Skel 1E 14
Poachers Ct. LN1: Sax 3E 8
Poachers Mdw. LN2: Nett 2C 12
Poachers Rest LN2: Welt 1C 4
Pocklington Cres. NG24: Wint 1H 35
Pocklington Rd. NG23: Coll 3J 33
Point, The LN6: Lin 2F 21
Policemans La. LN4: Wash 4E 18
Pompeii Ct. LN6: N Hyk 7H 21
Pond Cl. LN2: Welt 3C 4
  NG24: Bald 6K 37
Poplar Av. LN6: Lin 3C 16
Poplar Ct. LN6: Lin 3B 22
Poplar Farm Ct. LN2: Nett 1B 12
Poplars Gro. LN2: Lin 7K 11
Poplar St. LN5: Lin 2D 22
Poppleton Ho. LN6: Lin 3D 16
  (within The Pavilions Student Village)
Poppy Pl. NG24: N'wark T 6H 35
Portland Cl. NG24: N'wark T 7D 34
Portland St. LN5: Lin 7B 38 (4E 16)
  NG24: N'wark T 7D 34
Post Mill Cl. LN6: N Hyk 6G 21
Pottergate 3D 38 (2G 17)
Pottergate Cl. LN2: Lin 2D 38 (2F 17)
Pottergate Cl. LN5: Wad 2F 27
Pottergate Rd. LN5: Nav, Well 7J 31
POTTERHANWORTH 2A 28
Potterhanworth Rd. LN4: Bran, H'ton 7G 19
  LN4: Noct 6B 28
Potter Hill Rd. NG23: Coll 5J 33
Prebble Cl. NG24: N'wark T 4C 36
Prebend La. LN7: Welt 1B 4
Prenton Cl. LN6: Lin 2A 22
Preston Rd. NG24: N'wark T 7J 35
Prestwick Cl. LN6: Lin 5F 15
Prial Av. LN6: Lin 1B 22
Prial Cl. LN6: Lin 1B 22
Primrose Av. NG24: N'wark T 3F 35
Primrose Cl. LN5: Lin 5C 22
  LN6: N Hyk 7F 21
Prince Charles Av. LN8: Wrag 4G 7

Princess Margaret Av. LN4: Meth 5H 29
Princess Royal Cl. LN2: Lin 2G 17
Princess St. LN5: Lin 5D 16
Prince's St. LN4: Meth 5G 29
  NG24: N'wark T 1D 36
Prior La. LN4: Duns 4K 19
Prior St. LN5: Lin 7B 38 (5E 16)
Priory Cl. NG24: Bald 5H 37
Priory Dr. LN3: Fis 4K 19
Priorygate 2D 38 (2F 17)
Priorygate Ct. LN2: Lin 2D 38 (2F 17)
Priory Ho. LN5: Lin 7E 16
Private St. NG24: N'wark T 7F 35
Privet Wlk. LN6: With S 7A 26
Proctor M. LN6: Lin 3D 16
  (within The Pavilions Student Village)
Proctors Rd. LN2: Lin 1K 17
Providence Row LN3: L'worth 5C 6
Pudding Busk La. LN4: H'ton 1F 25
Pullan Cl. LN5: Lin 4D 22
Pullman Cl. LN4: Meth 5K 29
Putnam Dr. LN2: Lin 7K 11
Pyke Rd. LN6: Lin 2H 21
Pynder Cl. LN4: Wash 4C 18

Q

Quarry Ind. Estate, The LN5: Wad 2F 27
Queen Elizabeth Rd. LN1: Lin 5D 10
Queen Elizabeth St. LN8: Wrag 3G 7
Queen Headland La. LN5: Bass 5D 30
Queen Mary Rd. LN1: Lin 5D 10
Queensbury Ct. LN4: Wash 4D 18
Queen's Ct. NG24: N'wark T 6E 34
Queens Cres. LN1: Lin 1A 38 (1D 16)
Queens Farm Gdns. NG24: Bald 5H 37
Queen's Head Ct. NG24: N'wark T 7D 34
Queen's Rd. NG24: N'wark T 6D 34
Queen St. LN5: Lin 5E 16
  NG23: Coll 3H 33
  NG24: Bald 5J 37
  NG24: N'wark T 1C 36
Queensway LN1: Sax 3F 9
  LN2: Lin 1H 17
  LN4: Pott 1B 28
  LN6: Skel 3D 14
Queensway Ct. LN1: Sax 3F 9
Quibell Rd. NG24: N'wark T 3E 36
Quibell's La. NG24: N'wark T 4E 34
Quintin Cl. LN4: Brace H 4F 23
Quorn Dr. LN6: Lin 6C 16

R

RAF Waddington Golf Course 3J 27
Raglan Ct. NG24: N'wark T 1E 36
Raglan Gdns. NG24: N'wark T 1E 36
Raglan Ho. LN6: Lin 3D 16
Railway Ct. LN1: Sax 3E 8
Railway Pk. Cl. LN6: Lin 5D 16
Railway Pk. M. LN6: Lin 5D 16
Randall Cl. NG24: N'wark T 7H 35
Ransome Cl. NG24: N'wark T 7H 35
Rasen La. LN1: Lin 1B 38 (1E 16)
Rasuceby Ter. LN1: Lin 4A 38 (3E 16)
Ravendale Dr. LN2: Lin 6G 11
Ravensmoor Cl. LN6: N Hyk 7J 21
Raven's Vw. LN6: With S 7A 26
Ravenwood LN4: Wash 4C 18
Rayment Ho. LN6: Lin 1B 22
Raynton Cl. LN4: Wash 4C 18
Read Cl. NG24: Bald 6J 37
Reading Cl. LN4: Wash 5G 19
Rectory Cl. LN4: Pott 3A 28
Rectory La. LN4: Bran 4E 24
  LN5: Wad 3E 26
Redbourne Dr. LN2: Lin 5G 11
Redcar Cl. LN6: Lin 3K 21
Redcote Dr. LN6: Lin 3K 21
Red Hall Dr. LN4: Brace H 3F 23
Red Hall La. LN4: Brace H 3F 23
Redwing Cl. LN6: Skel 3E 14
Redwing Gro. LN6: Lin 6H 15
Redwood Dr. LN5: Wad 7C 22
Reed Dr. LN2: Lin 7K 11
REEPHAM 5H 13
Reepham Rd. LN3: Fis 6J 13
Regent Av. LN6: Lin 5G 15
Regents Cl. NG23: Coll 4J 33
Regents Cres. LN1: Lin 6E 10

Regents Pk. Cl. LN6: N Hyk 6K 21
Reid Ct. LN4: Bran .2E 24
Remigius Gro. LN2: Lin 6K 11
Remus Ct. LN6: N Hyk 7G 21
Renault Dr. LN4: Brace H 5F 23
Renfrew Cl. LN5: Lin 5C 22
Renfrew Rd. LN5: Lin 5C 22
Repton Cl. LN4: Wash 5F 19
Reservoir St. LN1: Lin 1B 38 (1E 16)
Restfil Way NG24: Bald 6K 37
Retief Cl. LN1: Lin .5D 10
Retief Vw. LN1: Lin 5D 10
Revesby Cl. LN4: Lin 1K 21
Revesby Sq. LN4: H'ton 7G 19
Reynolds Dr. LN6: Lin 1B 22
Reynolds Ho. LN6: Lin 1B 22
Richards Av. LN6: Lin 3K 21
Richmond Cl. NG24: New B 4F 37
Richmond Dr. LN6: N Hyk 4K 21
Richmond Gro. LN1: Lin 5D 10
Richmond Rd. LN1: Lin 2A 38 (2D 16)
Ridge Cl. LN2: Welt .2C 4
Ridge Vw. LN1: Lin 5D 10
   LN5: Harm 7E 26
Ridgeview Rd. LN4: Brace H 3F 23
Ridgeway LN2: Nett 2C 12
   LN4: Brace H 4G 23
Ridgewell Cl. LN6: Lin 6H 15
Ridings Cl. LN3: Fis 3K 19
Rigsmoor Cl. LN6: N Hyk 7J 21
Riley Cl. LN4: Brace H 5F 23
Ringrose Cl. NG24: N'wark T 7H 35
Ringwood Cl. LN6: Lin 5H 15
Rinks La. LN5: Bass 5B 30
Rio Dr. NG23: Coll .3H 33
Ripley Dr. LN4: Wash 4A 22
Ripon Cl. LN4: Brace H 3G 23
Ripon St. LN5: Lin 7C 38 (5F 17)
Risby Grn. LN6: Lin 7K 15
Rise, The LN5: Nav 5J 31
RISEHOLME 2G 11
Riseholme La. LN2: Nett, Ris 2F 11
Riseholme Rd. LN1: Lin 5F 11
Riseholme Rdbt. LN1: Burt Cl 4E 10
Riva Bingo
   Newark-on-Trent 7D 34
                     (within Castlegate Cen.)
Rivehall Av. LN2: Welt 1B 4
Riverdale LN2: Nett 1C 12
Rivermead LN6: Lin 3C 22
   NG24: N'wark T 3C 36
Rivermead Cl. LN6: Lin 3C 22
Riverside Apartments LN2: Lin 5D 38
Riverside Dr. LN5: Lin 7A 38 (4E 16)
Riverside Lawns LN5: Lin 5D 16
Riverside Pk. NG24: N'wark T 7B 34
Riverside Rd. NG24: N'wark T 3B 36
Riverton Cl. LN1: Lin 5D 10
Riverton Vw. LN1: Lin 5D 10
River Vw. NG24: N'wark T 5E 34
Robert Dukeson Av. NG24: N'wark T 3E 34
                                      (not continuous)
Robertson Cl. LN5: Wad 3F 27
Robertson Rd. LN6: N Hyk 6J 21
Robert Tressell Wlk. LN2: Lin 6J 11
Robey Ct. LN5: Lin .6E 16
Robey St. LN5: Lin .6E 16
Robin Hood Wlk. NG24: N'wark T 7D 34
Robins Ct. NG24: N'wark T 7E 34
Robins Cres. LN6: With S 6A 26
Robinson Cl. NG24: N'wark T 7J 35
Rochester Cl. LN4: Brace H 4G 23
Rochester Dr. LN6: Lin 1B 22
Rockingham Cl. LN6: Lin 7G 15
Rolleston Cl. LN2: Lin 6F 11
Roman Cl. LN4: Meth 5J 29
   LN5: Nav 4K 31
Roman Pavement LN2: Lin 2J 17
Roman Way LN6: S Hyk 7E 20
Roman Wharf LN1: Lin 2C 16
Romney Cl. LN6: Lin 1B 22
Romney Dr. LN6: Lin 1B 22
Romulus Way LN6: N Hyk 7G 21
Rookery, The LN2: Nett 5E 12
   NG23: Coll 3H 33
Rookery Cl. LN6: With S 7A 26
Rookery Ct. LN6: Lin 7C 16
Rookery La. LN6: Lin 1C 22
Rooks Cl. LN1: Sax .1F 9
Ropery, The LN1: Lin 3B 38 (2E 16)
Rope Wlk. LN1: Lin 6A 38 (4D 16)
Ropewalk LN8: Wrag 3H 7

Ropewalk, The NG24: N'wark T 7F 35
Rosebery Av. LN1: Lin 2D 16
Rosedale Cl. LN3: C Will 1G 19
   LN6: N Hyk 4K 21
Rosefield Cl. NG24: Bald 6K 37
Rosehill Cl. LN1: Sax 2E 8
Rose Hip Wlk. LN6: With S 7A 26
Roselea Av. LN2: Welt 2D 4
Rosemary Dr. LN6: With S 6B 26
Rosemary La. LN2: Lin 4D 38 (3F 17)
Roseum Cl. LN2: Lin 2J 21
Rosewood Cl. LN6: Lin 6G 15
   NG24: N'wark T 5F 35
Ross Cl. LN2: Lin 7K 11
Rossington Cl. LN4: Meth 4H 29
Rostrop Rd. LN4: Noct 5C 28
Rothwell Rd. LN2: Lin 6F 11
Roughton Ct. LN2: Lin 5G 11
Roundhead Building, The
   NG24: N'wark T 5E 34
                                         (off North Gate)
Routland Cl. LN8: Wrag 4H 7
Rowan Ct. LN4: H'ton 6F 19
Rowan Rd. LN5: Wad 6C 22
   LN6: N Hyk 4K 21
Rowans, The LN1: Sax 2D 8
   LN2: Nett 2B 12
Rowan Way LN4: Meth 4G 29
   NG24: New B 3F 37
Roxborough Cl. LN6: Lin 4J 15
Roxby Cl. LN6: Lin .1K 21
Royal Exchange Shop. Cen.
   NG24: N'wark T 7D 34
                                        (off Middle Ga.)
Royal Oak La. LN4: Wash 4E 18
Roydon Gro. LN6: Lin 7B 16
Ruby's Av. NG24: Bald 6J 37
Ruby's Wlk. NG24: Bald 6J 37
Ruckland Av. LN1: Lin 6E 10
Ruckland Ct. LN1: Lin 6E 10
Rudgard Av. LN3: C Will 7G 13
Rudgard Ho. LN6: Lin 3D 16
              (within The Pavilions Student Village)
Rudgard La. LN1: Lin 3A 38 (2D 16)
Rue De L'yonne NG23: Coll 2H 33
Rufford Av. NG24: N'wark T 1D 36
Rufford Grn. LN6: Lin 6C 16
Runcorn Rd. LN6: Lin 2F 21
Runswick Cl. LN6: N Hyk 4A 22
Rupert Cres. NG24: N'wark T 1D 36
Ruskin Av. LN2: Lin 7H 11
Ruskin Grn. LN2: Lin 7H 11
Rusland Cl. LN6: Lin 4G 11
Russell Av. LN6: N Hyk 7J 21
   NG24: New B 4F 37
Russell Ct. LN1: Lin 1C 38 (1F 17)
Russell St. LN5: Lin 1D 22
Ruston Way LN6: Lin 3D 16
Rutherglen Pk. LN1: Sax 1D 8
Rutland Av. NG24: N'wark T 2E 36
Rydal Cl. LN6: Lin .4H 15
Ryecroft LN6: Lin 5D 22
Ryland Bri. LN2: Welt 2D 4
Ryland Gdns. LN2: Welt 2D 4
Ryland Rd. LN2: Welt 2C 4
   LN2: Welt, Dunh .2D 4

S

Saddler's Cl. LN4: Meth 3H 29
Sadler Rd. LN6: Lin 1F 21
Sage Ct. LN6: Lin .6D 16
St Aiden's Rd. LN6: N Hyk 5H 21
St Albans Cl. LN4: Brace H 4G 23
St Andrew's Cl. LN5: Lin 5F 17
St Andrews Dr. LN1: Sax 2D 8
   LN6: Lin 6C 16
St Andrew's Gdns. LN6: Lin 6C 16
St Andrews Pl. LN5: Lin 7D 38 (4F 17)
St Andrew's St. LN5: Lin 7D 38 (5F 17)
St Annes Bedehouses LN2: Lin 2H 17
St Annes Cl. LN2: Lin 2H 17
St Annes Rd. LN2: Lin 2H 17
St Aubins Cres. LN4: H'ton 7G 19
St Augustine Rd. LN2: Lin 7B 12
St Augustine's Cl. NG24: N'wark T 1F 37
                                       (off Newton St.)
ST BARNABAS HOSPICE 1E 38 (1F 17)
St Benedicts Cl. LN6: N Hyk 5H 21
St Benedict's Sq. LN5: Lin 5B 38 (3E 16)
St Botolphs Cl. LN1: Sax 1F 9

St Botolph's Ct. LN5: Lin 6E 16
St Botolph's Cres. LN5: Lin 6D 16
St Botolphs Ga. LN1: Sax 1E 8
ST CATHERINES 7D 16
St Catherines LN5: Lin 7E 16
St Catherines Cl. NG24: N'wark T 1C 36
St Catherine's Ct. LN5: Lin 7D 16
St Catherine's Gro. LN5: Lin 7D 16
St Catherines M. LN5: Lin 7D 16
                                       (off St Catherines)
St Catherine's Rd. LN5: Lin 7E 16
St Catherine's Ter. LN5: Lin 7D 16
St Chad's Ct. LN2: Dunh 3F 5
St Claire's Ct. LN6: Lin 6G 15
St Clare's Ga. NG24: N'wark T 2E 36
St Clements Cl. LN1: Lin 1C 38
St Clement's Dr. LN3: Fis 4K 19
St Clements Pas. LN2: Lin 4E 38 (3G 17)
St Clements Rd. LN6: N Hyk 5J 21
St Crispin's Cl. LN6: N Hyk 5H 21
St Cuthberts Cl. LN2: Lin 3C 38
St David's Cl. LN3: C Will 6G 13
St Davids Rd. LN6: N Hyk 5H 21
St Edward's Dr. LN2: Scot 1J 11
St Faith's Ct. LN1: Lin 3A 38 (2D 16)
St Faith's St. LN1: Lin 3A 38 (2D 16)
St Francis's Ct. LN6: N Hyk 5H 21
St George's Cl. LN6: N Hyk 4J 21
St George's Ct. NG24: N'wark T 6E 34
St George's La. LN3: Ris 4F 11
St George's M. LN1: Sax 2D 8
ST GILES 6H 11
St Giles Av. LN2: Lin 1E 38 (1G 17)
St Gile's Way NG24: Bald 4J 37
St Helen's Av. LN6: Lin 7B 16
St Hilarys Cl. LN6: N Hyk 4H 21
St Hugh's Cl. LN3: C Will 6G 13
St Hugh's Dr. LN3: L'worth 5C 6
   LN6: N Hyk 5J 21
St Hugh St. LN2: Lin 4E 38 (3G 17)
St James Pl. LN6: N Hyk 4J 21
St Johns Av. LN3: C Will 6G 13
St Johns Rd. LN1: Lin 7F 11
   LN4: Brace H 4F 23
St John's Sq. LN4: Brace H 4G 23
                                      (not continuous)
St Katherine's 900 Years of History,
   Heritage and Cultural Cen. 6E 16
St Leonard's Ct. NG24: N'wark T 6D 34
                                        (off Kirk Ga.)
St Leonard's La. LN2: Lin 2E 38 (2G 17)
St Luke's Cl. LN3: C Will 6H 13
St Margaret's Cl. LN2: Lin 3B 22
St Margaret's Gdns. LN6: Lin 3A 22
St Mark's LN6: Lin 6A 38 (4D 16)
                                      (not continuous)
St Mark's Av. LN3: C Will 6G 13
St Marks Cl. LN6: N Hyk 4J 21
St Mark's La. NG24: N'wark T 7D 34
                                      (not continuous)
St Mark's Pl. NG24: N'wark T 7D 34
St Marks Shop. Pk. LN5: Lin 6B 38 (4E 16)
   LN6: Lin 6A 38 (4E 16)
St Mark's Sq. LN5: Lin 6A 38 (4E 16)
St Mark St. LN5: Lin 6B 38 (4E 16)
St Martin's La. LN2: Lin 3C 38 (2F 17)
St Martin's St. LN2: Lin 3C 38 (2F 17)
St Mary's Av. LN2: Welt 1C 4
St Mary's Ct. NG24: N'wark T 7E 34
St Mary's Gdns. NG24: N'wark T 3C 36
St Marys Rd. LN6: N Hyk 5J 21
St Mary's St. LN5: Lin 6B 38 (4F 17)
St Matthews Cl. LN3: C Will 6G 13
St Michael Cl. LN5: Wad 3F 27
St Michaels Ter. LN1: Lin 3C 38 (2F 17)
St Nicholas St. LN1: Lin 1B 38 (1F 17)
St Paul's Av. LN3: C Will 6G 13
St Pauls Cl. LN5: Wad 3F 27
St Paul's La. LN1: Lin 2C 38 (2F 17)
St Peter at Arches LN2: Lin 4C 38
St Peters Av. LN3: C Will 6G 13
   LN6: Lin 2C 22
   LN6: N Hyk 5H 21
St Rumbold's St. LN2: Lin 5D 38 (3F 17)
St Simon's Dr. LN3: C Will 6G 13
St Stephen's Ct. LN6: N Hyk 6J 21
St Swithin's Sq. LN2: Lin 5C 38 (3F 17)
St Wilfreds Rd. NG23: N Mus 4C 32
St Wilfrid's Cl. LN4: Meth 5J 29
Salisbury Cl. LN1: Sax 2E 8

Salisbury Dr. LN4: Brace H 3G 23
Salisbury Rd. NG24: N'wark T 2D 36
Salix App. LN6: Lin 5G 15
Saltergate LN2: Lin 5C 38 (3F 17)
Salters Cl. LN4: Brace H 5G 23
Sam Derry Cl. NG24: N'wark T 7F 35
Sanders Cl. LN1: Lin 5D 10
Sanders Vw. LN1: Lin 5D 10
Sandfield Way NG24: N'wark T 3B 36
Sandhills Cl. NG24: N'wark T 6C 34
Sandhill Sconce NG24: N'wark T 7B 34
Sandhills Pk. NG24: N'wark T 6C 34
Sandra Cres. LN4: Wash 5F 19
Sandtoft Cl. LN6: Lin 1H 21
Sandwell Dr. LN6: Lin 5H 15
Sanigar Ct. NG24: N'wark T 5G 35
Sansford Grn. LN6: Lin 1A 22
Sapling Cl. NG24: New B 3G 37
Saracen's Head Yd. NG24: N'wark T 7D 34
Sargent Cl. LN4: Meth 4G 29
Sastangate Ho. LN1: Lin 1B 38 (1E 16)
Satinwood Cl. LN6: Lin 5G 15
Satterley Cl. LN6: With S 7B 26
Saucemere Dr. NG24: N'wark T 2D 36
Sausthorpe Ct. LN5: Lin 5F 17
Sausthorpe St. LN5: Lin 5F 17
Saville St. LN5: Lin 7D 16
Savoy Ct. NG24: N'wark T 7D 34
Sawmill La. LN8: Wrag 3F 7
Sawyers Cl. NG24: N'wark T 7F 35
SAXILBY 3E 8
Saxilby Ent. Pk. LN1: Sax 4H 9
Saxilby Rd. LN1: Bro 5E 8
  LN1: Burt L, Lin . . . . .4K 9, 6H 9 & 6A 10
  LN6: Skel 1E 14
Saxilby Station (Rail) 3E 8
Saxon Cl. LN4: Meth 5J 29
Saxon St. LN1: Lin 1B 38 (1E 16)
Saxon Vs. LN1: Lin 1E 16
Scampton Av. LN6: Lin 1K 21
Scarle Cl. LN6: Lin 5A 22
Scawby Cres. LN6: Lin 7K 15
Schoeffer Ho. LN6: Lin 6F 15
School Cres. LN2: Scot 6G 5
School Dr. LN2: Welt 2B 4
School La. LN1: Bro 7A 8
  LN4: Can 6G 17
  LN4: Wash .4E 18
  LN5: Harm .7E 26
  LN6: N Hyk .6K 21
  LN6: T Hill 7B 20
  NG23: Thor 7A 8
School Rd. LN4: Noct 6B 28
Sconce Wlk. NG24: N'wark T 2C 36
Scopwick Pl. LN2: Lin 5F 11
Scorer St. LN5: Lin 5E 16
SCOTHERN 7H 5
Scothern La. LN2: Dunh 3E 4
  LN2: Scot 1G 13
  LN3: L'worth .4C 6
  LN3: Stain L .2B 6
Scothern Rd. LN2: Nett . . . . . . .1B 12 & 7D 4
Scott Gdns. LN2: Lin 7J 11
Scotton Dr. LN6: Lin 7A 16
Seacroft NG24: N'wark T 7J 35
Searby Rd. LN2: Lin 5H 11
Sedgebrook Cl. LN2: Lin 5F 11
Sedgebrook Ho. LN2: Lin 5F 11
Sedgemoor Cl. LN6: N Hyk 6J 21
Seely Cl. LN4: H'ton 6F 19
Selby Cl. LN6: N Hyk 4A 22
Sempers Cl. LN6: T Hill 7B 20
Seven Hills NG24: N'wark T 4E 34
Severn St. LN1: Lin 2C 16
Severus Cres. LN6: N Hyk 7H 21
Sewell Rd. LN2: Lin 2G 17
Sewells Wlk. LN5: Lin 5E 16
Sewstern Cl. LN4: Brace H 5G 23
Shaftesbury Av. LN6: Lin 4H 15
Shaftesbury Way NG23: Coll 3H 33
Shakespeare St. LN5: Lin 6E 16
  NG24: New B 2F 37
Shamrock Cotts. LN5: Lin 1E 22
Shamrock Cl. LN5: Lin 1E 22
Shannon Av. LN6: Lin 2A 22
Shannon Cl. LN6: Lin 2A 22
Shardloes LN4: Bran 3F 25
Sharp Wlk. LN6: N Hyk 7K 21
Shawbury Cl. LN6: Lin 1G 21

Shaw Way LN2: Nett 1B 12
Shays Dr. LN6: Lin 7A 16
Shearwater Cl. LN6: Lin 5J 15
Shearwater Rd. LN6: Lin 6J 15
Sheepwalk LN6: With S 4B 26
Sheepwash La. LN4: H'ton 6E 18
Sheldrake Rd. NG24: N'wark T 7H 35
Shelley Cl. NG24: Bald 5H 37
Shelley Dr. LN2: Lin 7H 11
Shelton Av. NG24: N'wark T 3C 36
Shepherds Way LN2: Scot 1H 13
Sheppard Ct. LN4: Brace H 4G 23
Sheppard's Cl. LN4: H'ton 6E 18
Sheraton Cl. LN6: Lin 7H 15
Sherbrooke St. LN2: Lin 3K 17
Sheridan Cl. LN2: Lin 6J 11
  NG24: Bald .4H 37
Sherwood Av. NG24: N'wark T 1E 36
Sherwood Dr. LN5: Wad 6D 22
Shiregate LN4: Meth 3H 29
Shirley Av. LN4: Duns 2F 29
Short Furrow LN5: Nav 5K 31
Short Wheatley La. NG23: Coll 7H 33
Shuttleworth Ct. LN6: N Hyk 7J 21
Shuttleworth Ho. LN2: Lin 3G 17
Sibcy La. NG24: Bald 5H 37
Sibthorpe Dr. LN2: Scot 1H 13
Sibthorp Gdns. LN4: Can 6H 17
Sibthorp St. LN5: Lin 7B 38 (5E 16)
Side Row NG24: N'wark T 7F 35
Sidings, The LN1: Sax 3E 8
  LN6: Lin 6A 38 (4E 16)
Sidlaw Gro. LN5: Lin 5C 22
Sidney St. LN5: Lin 6E 16
Sidney Ter. LN5: Lin 6E 16
Sikorski Cl. NG24: N'wark T 6D 34
Silverstone Rd. LN6: Lin 7G 15
Silver St. LN2: Lin 4C 38 (3F 17)
  LN4: Bran 4E 24
  LN8: Wrag 3H 7
Simon's Grn. LN6: Lin 1C 22
Simpson Cl. NG24: Bald 5J 37
Sincil Bank LN5: Lin 7C 38 (6E 16)
Sincil Bank Stadium 5F 17
Sincil St. LN5: Lin 6C 38 (5F 17)
Sinderson Mdws. LN6: S Hyk 7E 20
Sixfield Cl. LN6: Lin 7A 16
Skayman Flds. LN5: Carl M 7B 30
SKELLINGTHORPE 2E 14
Skellingthorpe Heritage Room 2F 15
Skellingthorpe Rd. LN1: Sax 3F 9
  LN6: Lin 4H 15
Skellingthorpe Rdbt. LN6: Lin 4G 15
Skerries Cl. LN6: N Hyk 6K 21
SKEWBRIDGE 5D 16
Skinnand La. LN5: Well 7F 31
Skipwith Cres. LN4: Meth 5J 29
Skirbeck Dr. LN1: Sax 3E 8
Slake La. NG23: S Mus 1C 34
Slaughter Ho. La. NG24: N'wark T 6D 34
Sleaford Rd. LN4: Brace H 4G 23
  LN4: Bran, Pott 4E 24
  LN4: Duns, Meth 1F 29
  LN5: Well 6H 31
  NG24: N'wark T 6E 34
Slessor St. LN5: Wad 1D 22
Smith Ho. NG24: N'wark T 4D 36
Smithson Cl. NG24: New B 4G 37
Smith St. LN5: Lin 5E 16
  NG24: New B 3G 37
  NG24: N'wark T 1E 36
Smithy Yd. LN8: Wrag 3G 7
Smooting La. LN3: Ree 5J 13
Smoots, The LN5: Nav 4J 31
Smythson Grn. LN6: Dodd 5A 14
Snaith Cl. LN6: Lin 1F 21
Snaith Ct. NG24: N'wark T 6D 34
Snetterton Cl. LN6: Lin 7G 15
Snowberry Gdns. LN6: Lin 6G 15
Snowdon Cl. LN5: Lin 4D 22
Snowdon Rd. NG23: Coll 4H 33
Snowdrop Av. NG24: N'wark T 6J 35
Sobraon Hgts. LN1: Lin 6E 10
Somersby Cl. LN6: Lin 3C 22
Somerset Ho. LN2: Lin 5F 11
Somerton Ga. La. LN5: Wad 3B 22
Somerton Ri. LN5: Booth G 1J 31
Somerville Cl. LN5: Wad 1D 26
Somerville Cl. LN5: Wad 1D 26
Somme Cl. LN1: Lin 6E 10
Sorrel Ct. LN6: Lin 6G 15
Sorrel Rd. LN6: With S 7A 26

Southcote M. LN6: Lin 3K 21
Southdown LN5: Lin 6D 22
South End NG23: Coll 5G 33
Southend Av. NG24: N'wark T 1D 36
Southfield NG24: Bald 5J 37
Southfield Ho. NG24: N'wark T 1C 36
Southfield Ter. NG24: N'wark T 1C 36
Southland Dr. LN6: Lin 3B 22
SOUTH MUSKHAM 7B 32
South Pde. LN1: Lin 3A 38 (2D 16)
  LN1: Sax 2E 8
South Pk. LN5: Lin 6E 16
South Pk. Av. LN5: Lin 6F 17
Sth. Scaffold La. NG23: Coll 7J 33
Sth. Scarle Rd. NG23: Coll 2J 33
South Vw. LN2: Dunh 3F 5
  NG24: New B 4G 37
Southwell Cl. LN4: Brace H 3H 23
Spa Bldgs. LN2: Lin 4D 38 (3F 17)
Spanby Dr. LN6: Lin 7A 16
Spa Rd. LN2: Lin 3H 17
Sparrow La. LN2: Lin 5E 38 (3G 17)
Spa St. LN2: Lin .3H 17
Speedwell Cl. NG24: N'wark T 6J 35
Speight Cl. NG24: Wint 1G 35
Spencer Cl. LN1: Sax 3G 9
Spencer St. LN5: Lin 6E 16
Spennymoor Cl. LN6: N Hyk 7H 21
Sperrin Cl. LN5: Lin 5D 22
Spilsby Cl. LN6: Lin 6H 15
Spinney, The NG24: Wint 2G 35
Spinney Cl. NG24: N'wark T 2C 36
Spinneys, The LN2: Welt 1C 4
Spirea App. LN6: Lin 6G 15
Spire Cl. LN1: Lin 6E 10
Spire Gdns. NG24: N'wark T 4F 35
Spital St. LN1: Lin 7F 11
Spring Cl. LN2: Dunh 3F 5
Spring Ct. LN2: Welt 1C 4
  LN4: Duns 2H 29
Spring Dr. NG24: Bald 6K 37
Springfield Cl. LN1: Lin 1F 17
  LN4: Bran 4E 24
Spring Gdns. NG24: N'wark T 1C 36
Spring Hill LN1: Lin 3B 38 (2E 16)
  LN3: Ree 5H 13
Spring La. NG24: Bald 4J 37
  (Gamage Cl.)
  NG24: Bald .5K 37
  (Hollowdyke La.)
Spruce Cres. LN4: Bran 3D 24
Spurr, The LN5: Well 6J 31
Squires Pl. LN2: Nett 2C 12
Squirrel Chase LN6: With S 6A 26
Stable Yard, The LN2: Nett 2B 12
Stafford Av. NG24: New B 4G 37
Staffordshire Cres. LN6: Lin 7H 15
STAINTON BY LANGWORTH 2C 6
Stainton Gdns. LN1: Lin 6E 10
Stainton La. LN2: Scot 6K 5
  LN3: New, Stain L 2C 6
Stamp End LN2: Lin 5E 38 (3G 17)
Standish Ho. NG24: N'wark T 4E 36
Stane Dr. LN4: Brace H 5G 23
Stanhope Av. NG24: N'wark T 3G 35
Stanley Cres. LN4: Brace H 3F 23
Stanley Pl. LN5: Lin 5F 17
Stanley St. LN5: Lin 7D 16
  NG24: N'wark T 6F 35
Stanley Ter. NG24: N'wark T 7F 35
Stanthaket Ct. LN1: Lin 3B 38 (2F 17)
Stapleford Av. LN2: Lin 5F 11
Staple La. NG24: Bald 7F 37
Staples La. LN5: Wad 3E 26
Stark Way LN2: Lin 7K 11
Starr's Yd. NG24: N'wark T 7D 34
  (off Mill Ga.)
Station App. LN1: Sax 3E 8
Station Cl. NG23: Coll 5J 33
Station Fld. LN6: Skel 3F 15
Station Rd. LN3: L'worth 6A 6
  LN3: Ree 5H 13
  LN4: Bran 4E 24
  LN4: H'ton 7F 19
  LN4: Meth 4J 29
  LN4: Pott 7H 25
  LN5: Harm 7D 26
  LN5: Wad 1C 26
  LN6: N Hyk .4H 21
  LN6: T Hill 6A 20
  NG23: Coll .4H 33
  NG23: Harby .7D 8

Station St. LN5: Lin 6B 38 (4E 16)
Staunton Ct. LN1: Lin 3D 16
Staunton Rd. NG24: N'wark T 3D 36
Staunton St. LN1: Lin 3D 16
(not continuous)
Staverton Cres. LN6: Lin 6F 15
Steamer Point Rd. LN4: Noct 5C 28
Steeles Dr. NG24: Bald 4J 37
Steepers, The LN2: Nett 1C 12
Steep Hill LN2: Lin 3C 38 (2F 17)
Steeping Cl. LN1: Lin 5E 10
Stenigot Cl. LN6: Lin 1G 21
Stenigot Gro. LN6: Lin 1H 21
Stenigot Rd. LN6: Lin 1G 21
Stephen Rd. NG24: N'wark T 3F 35
Stephenson Ct. NG24: N'wark T 4G 35
Stephenson Rd. LN6: N Hyk 3H 21
Stephenson Way NG24: N'wark T 4G 35
Stevenson Cl. LN4: H'ton 7F 19
Stewards Way LN4: Brace H 4G 23
Stewart Cl. LN2: Welt 1D 4
Stewart's Yd. LN5: Lin 5C 38
Stirling Dr. NG24: Codd 5J 35
Stirling Way LN6: Skel 2D 14
Stocking Way LN2: Lin 7B 12
Stodman M. NG24: N'wark T 7D 34
Stodman St. NG24: N'wark T 7D 34
Stoke Av. NG24: N'wark T 7D 34
Stonebow Cen. LN2: Lin 4C 38
Stonecliff Pk. LN2: Welt 1B 4
Stonefield Av. LN2: Lin 1D 38 (1F 17)
Stone La. LN5: Wad 2F 27
Stonelea Cl. LN4: Bran 4F 25
Stone Moor Rd. LN6: N Hyk 7J 21
Stones La. LN6: Lin 5J 15
Stone Valley Ct. LN5: Wad 2F 27
Stoney Yd. LN6: Skel 1E 14
Stoyles Way LN4: H'ton 6F 19
Strahane Cl. LN5: Lin 5C 38
Strait, The LN2: Lin 3C 38 (2F 17)
Strawberry Hall La. NG24: N'wark T 5F 35
Strubby Cl. LN6: Lin 6H 15
Stuart Ho. LN2: Lin 6G 11
Stukeley Cl. LN2: Lin 7A 12
Stukeley Ct. NG24: N'wark T 5F 35
Sturgate Cl. LN6: Lin 7G 15
Sturton Cl. LN2: Lin 6F 11
Sturton Rd. LN1: Sax 1F 9
Sudbeck La. LN2: Welt 2C 4
SUDBROOKE 1H 13
Sudbrooke Dr. LN2: Lin 6G 11
Sudbrooke La. LN2: Nett, Scot 2C 12
Sudbrooke Rd. LN2: Scot 7G 5
Sudbury Cl. LN4: Lin 2A 22
Summers Rd. NG24: N'wark T 5E 34
Sunbeam Av. LN6: N Hyk 6H 21
Sunderland Cl. LN6: Skel 2E 14
Sunfield Cres. LN6: Lin 5H 15
Sunningdale Dr. LN6: Lin 6D 16
Sunningdale Gro. LN4: H'ton 5F 19
Sunningdale Trad. Est. LN6: Lin 5C 16
Superbowl
Lincoln 4C 16
Sutton Av. NG24: N'wark T 4C 36
Sutton Cl. LN2: Nett 2A 12
LN4: Wash 5C 18
Swaby Cl. LN2: Lin 5G 11
Swallow Av. LN6: Skel 3E 14
SWALLOW BECK .3K 21
Swallowbeck Av. LN6: Lin 3K 21
Swallowbeck Ct. LN6: Lin 3K 21
Swallow Dr. LN8: Wrag 4G 7
Swallow Gdns. LN6: Lin 3K 21
Swan Cl. LN2: Dunh 3E 4
Swanholme Cl. LN6: Lin 2J 21
Swanholme Lakes Local Nature Reserve . .1J 21
Swanpool Ct. LN5: Lin 5B 38
SWANPOOL GARDEN SUBURB 6A 16
Swan St. LN2: Lin 4C 38 (1D 16)
Swayne Cl. LN2: Lin 6K 11
Swaythling Cl. LN6: Lin 2J 21
Swen Cl. LN2: Welt 1D 4
Swift Gdns. LN2: Lin 6H 11
Swift Grn. LN2: Lin 6H 11
Swinburne Cl. NG24: Bald 3H 37
Swinderby Cl. NG24: N'wark T 6H 35
Swinderby Rd. NG23: Coll 4H 33
Sycamore Cl. LN3: C Will 1F 19
LN4: Bran 2D 24
LN6: Lin 6J 15
NG24: Hawt 5B 36
NG24: N'wark T 3D 36
Sycamore Cres. LN6: Lin 6J 15

Sycamore Dr. LN5: Wad 7C 22
Sycamore Gro. LN4: Brace H 5G 23
Sydney St. NG24: N'wark T 6E 34
Sydney Ter. NG24: N'wark T 1E 36
Syd Wilson Ct. LN1: Lin 6D 10
Syerston Way NG24: N'wark T 6H 35
Sykes La. LN1: Sax 1B 8
NG24: Bald 4H 37
Sympson Cl. LN2: Lin 6A 12
Syringa Grn. LN6: Lin 5G 15
Syston Gro. LN5: Lin 3D 22
Sywell Cl. LN6: Lin 1G 21

T

Talbot Cl. LN5: Nav 4J 31
Tall Pines Rd. LN6: With S 7A 26
Tamar Way LN6: N Hyk 5A 22
Tangshan Cl. LN1: Lin 5E 10
Tankard Building, The NG24: N'wark T 5E 34
(off North Gate)
Tanner's Ct. LN5: Lin 7A 38
Tanner's La. LN5: Lin 7B 38 (4E 16)
Tannery Wharf NG24: N'wark T 7C 34
Tapin Cl. LN1: Lin .7C 10
Taurus Av. LN6: N Hyk 7G 21
Tealby St. LN5: Lin 6E 16
Tedder Dr. LN5: Wad 2F 27
Teesdale Cl. LN6: Lin 4G 15
Telford Ct. NG24: N'wark T 4G 35
Telford Dr. NG24: N'wark T 4G 35
Temperance La. NG23: Coll 4G 33
Tempest St. LN2: Lin 3H 17
Temple Gdns. LN2: Lin 3D 38 (2F 17)
Temple Goring LN5: Nav 5K 31
Ten Acre La. LN4: H'ton 2G 25
Tennyson Cl. LN4: Meth 4H 29
Tennyson Dr. LN2: Dunh 3D 4
Tennyson Ho. LN2: Dunh 3D 4
Tennyson Rd. NG24: Bald 4H 37
Tennyson St. LN1: Lin 2D 16
Tennyson Wlk. LN3: C Will 7E 12
Tentercroft St. LN5: Lin 6B 38 (4E 16)
Tentercroft St. Ind. Est. LN5: Lin . . .6C 38 (4F 17)
Tenter La. LN5: Nav 4J 31
Tenzing Wlk. NG24: Bald 4J 37
Terry Av. NG24: N'wark T 4F 35
Terry O Toole Theatre 6H 21
Tetney Cl. LN1: Lin 5E 10
Thackers La. LN4: Bran 4E 24
The . . . .
Names prefixed with 'The' for example
'The Alders' are indexed under the main
name such as 'Alders, The'
Theatre Royal
Lincoln 4C 38
Theodore St. LN1: Lin 1A 38 (1E 16)
Theresa Ct. NG24: Bald 4H 37
Thesiger Ct. LN5: Lin 5F 17
(off Thesiger St.)
Thesiger St. LN5: Lin 5F 17
Third Hill Rd. LN4: H'ton 1H 25
Thirlmere Cl. LN6: N Hyk 5A 22
Thirlmere Way LN6: Lin 4G 15
Thirsk Dr. LN6: Lin 3K 21
Thistle Cl. LN2: Lin 5J 11
Thomas Ct. LN2: Lin 3G 17
(off Thomas St.)
Thomas Pl. NG23: N Mus 5C 32
Thomas Rd. NG24: Bald 6K 37
Thomas St. LN2: Lin 3G 17
Thompson Cl. NG24: Codd 5J 35
Thonock Cl. LN1: Lin 6F 11
Thonock Dr. LN1: Sax 2D 8
Thoresby Av. NG24: N'wark T 2E 36
Thoresway Dr. LN2: Lin 6G 11
Thorngate LN2: Lin 5C 38 (3F 17)
Thorngate Ho. LN2: Lin 5D 38
(off St Swithin's Sq.)
Thornton Cl. LN4: Wash 4C 18
LN6: Lin 7A 16
Thornton Rd. NG23: Coll 4H 33
Thornton Way LN3: C Will 7G 13
Thorold Way LN5: Harm 7E 26
Thoroton Av. NG24: Bald 5H 37
Thoroughfare La. NG24: Wint 1H 35
Thorpe Av. LN1: Lin 6D 10
Thorpe Cl. NG24: N'wark T 4C 36
Thorpe La. LN6: S Hyk 7E 20
THORPE ON THE HILL 7B 20
Thorpe Park Golf Course 7C 20
Thorpe Pk. Lodges LN6: T Hill 7C 20

Thorpe Rd. LN6: Whi 5A 20
Thorsby Cl. LN5: Wad 6D 22
Thurlby Cl. LN4: Wash 4C 18
Thurlby Cres. LN2: Lin 5H 11
Thurlby Rd. LN5: Bass 2C 30
Thurlow Ct. LN2: Lin 6A 12
Thyme Ct. LN6: Lin 6D 16
Thyme Wlk. LN6: With S 6B 26
Tiber Rd. LN6: N Hyk 7G 21
Timms La. LN5: Wad 3E 26
Tinkermere Cl. LN2: Welt 2C 4
Tinker's La. LN5: Wad 4E 26
Tithe Barn Ct. NG24: N'wark T 6E 34
Tobruk Cl. LN1: Lin 5D 10
Tolney La. NG24: N'wark T 7B 34
Tom Otter's La. LN1: Sax 5B 8
NG23: Harby 5B 8
Tom Ward Cl. LN1: Lin 7F 11
Top Lodge Cl. LN6: Lin 2J 21
Top Row NG24: N'wark T 7G 35
Torgate Av. LN5: Bass 3D 30
Torgate La. LN5: Bass 3D 30
Torksey Av. LN1: Sax 2D 8
Toronto St. LN2: Lin 3J 17
Torrington Rd. LN2: Lin 5F 11
Total Fitness
Lincoln 2F 21
Tothill Cl. LN6: Lin 7K 15
Tourist Info. Cen.
Lincoln 2C 38 (2F 17)
Newark-on-Trent 6D 34
Tower Av. LN2: Lin 2K 17
LN4: Brace H 4F 23
Tower Cres. LN2: Lin 2K 17
Tower Dr. LN2: Lin 2K 17
Tower Flats LN2: Lin 2K 17
Tower Gdns. LN2: Lin 2K 17
Tower La. LN4: Brace H 7H 27
Town Hall Museum & Art Gallery 7D 34
Townhill Sq. NG24: Bald 6K 37
Townsend Way LN4: Meth 5H 29
Toynton Cl. LN6: Lin 3B 22
Trafalgar Cl. LN4: Wash 4D 18
Trelawney Cres. LN1: Lin 5E 10
Trelawney Ho. LN1: Lin 5E 10
Trenchard Sq. LN5: Wad 2G 27
Trent Cl. NG23: N Mus 4C 32
Trent La. NG23: Kel, S Mus 2A 34
NG24: N'wark T 5E 34
Trentside Bus. Village
NG24: N'wark T 2A 36
Trent Vw. LN1: Lin 6D 10
Trent Vs. NG24: N'wark T 2A 36
Trent Way NG24: N'wark T 5F 35
Trevose Dr. LN6: N Hyk 6K 21
Trinity Cl. LN5: Carl M 7C 30
Trinity Rd. NG24: N'wark T 4E 36
Tritton Retail Pk. LN6: Lin 4D 16
Tritton Rd. LN6: Lin 3K 21
Tritton Rd. Trad. Est. LN6: Lin 5C 16
Trollope St. LN5: Lin 7C 38 (4F 17)
Troon Cl. LN4: Wash 5F 19
Troutbeck Cl. LN2: Lin 5G 11
Truro Dr. LN6: Lin .6F 15
Tryst, The NG24: N'wark T 5E 34
Tudor Cl. NG24: N'wark T 7F 35
Tudor Ho. LN2: Lin 5G 11
Tudor Rd. LN6: Lin 1H 21
Tulipwood Av. LN6: Lin 5G 15
Turnberry Cl. LN4: H'ton 6F 19
Turnbury Cl. LN6: Lin 7F 15
Turner Av. LN6: Lin 1A 22
Turner Cl. LN5: Nav 4K 31
Turner Ct. LN6: Lin 6K 15
Turner St. LN1: Lin 1A 38 (1E 16)
Turner Cl. LN8: Wrag 3G 7
Tutt Cl. NG24: Bald 6K 37
Twenty Row LN5: Nav 3K 31
Twitchell, The NG24: N'wark T 3C 36
Tyne Cl. LN6: N Hyk 5A 22

U

Uffington Av. LN6: Lin 1A 22
Uffington Cl. LN6: Lin 7A 16
UK Superbowl
Newark-on-Trent 7D 34
(within Castlegate Cen.)
Uldale Cl. LN6: Lin 4G 15
Ullswater Cl. LN6: N Hyk 5A 22
Union Rd. LN1: Lin 2B 38 (2F 16)
Unity Sq. LN2: Lin 4D 38 (3F 17)

University of Lincoln—Willingham Av.

University of Lincoln
Brayford Campus 5A 38
Cathedral Campus -
Lindum Rd. 3D 38 (2F 17)
Wordsworth St. 3C 38
Danesgate House 4C 38
Riseholme Campus 1H 11
Thomas Parker House 4C 38
Up. Lindum St. LN2: Lin 3E 38 (2G 17)
Up. Long Leys Rd. LN1: Lin 1A 38 (1E 16)
Up. Saxon St. LN1: Lin 1E 16
Urban St. LN5: Lin 1D 22
Usher Av. LN6: Lin 7B 16
Usher Gallery 3D 38
Usher Grn. LN6: Lin 1B 22

V

Valentine Pk. Sth. LN6: Lin 5C 16
Valentine Retail Pk. LN6: Lin 5C 16
Valentine Rd. LN6: Lin 5C 16
Vale Vw. NG24: N'wark T 3B 36
Valiant St. LN5: Wad 3G 27
Valley Prospect NG24: N'wark T 2B 36
Valley Rd. LN5: Wad 7C 22
Vanwall Dr. LN5: Wad 2F 27
Vasey Cl. LN1: Sax 3G 9
Vauxhall Rd. LN4: Brace H 5F 23
Venables Ct. LN2: Lin 7K 11
Venables Way LN2: Lin 7K 11
Ventnor Ter. LN2: Lin 3C 38
Verdun Cl. LN1: Lin 6E 10
Vere St. LN1: Lin 7F 11
Vernon Av. NG24: N'wark T 7F 35
Vernon St. LN5: Lin 5D 16
NG24: N'wark T 7F 35
Veronica Cl. LN4: Bran 3D 24
Vessey Cl. NG24: New B 4G 37
Vicarage Cl. NG23: Coll 3H 33
Vicarage Ct. LN5: Lin 5F 17
Vicarage Dr. LN6: Skel 3F 15
Vicarage Gdns. NG24: Bald 4J 37
Vicarage La. LN2: Nett 2B 12
LN2: Scot 7G 5
LN2: Welt 2C 4
LN4: Duns 2G 29
LN5: Carl M 6C 30
LN5: Harm 6E 26
LN5: Well 6H 31
NG23: N Mus 2A 32
Vicar's Ct. LN2: Lin 3D 38 (2F 17)
Victor Dr. LN6: N Hyk 6G 21
Victoria Gdns. NG24: N'wark T 7E 34
Victoria Gro. LN4: Wash 5F 19
Victoria Pas. LN1: Lin 3A 38 (2E 16)
Victoria Pl. LN1: Lin 3B 38 (2E 16)
Victoria St. LN1: Lin 3B 38 (2E 16)
LN5: Lin 2D 22
LN8: Wrag 3G 7
NG24: N'wark T 1C 36
Victoria Ter. LN1: Lin 3A 38 (2E 16)
NG24: N'wark T 7D 34
Victor Way LN5: Wad 3G 27
Vigo Cl. LN1: Lin 6C 10
Viking Cl. LN5: Wad 2E 26
Viking Ct. LN4: Brace H 4F 23
Viking Way LN4: Meth 5H 29
Villa Cl. LN4: Bran 4E 24
Village Farm LN5: Bass 2D 30
Vindex Cl. LN1: Lin 7D 10
Vine Farm Yd. NG23: Coll 3H 33
Vine St. LN2: Lin 4E 38 (3G 17)
Vine Way NG24: N'wark T 7F 35
Vixen Cl. NG24: N'wark T 4D 36
Vulcan Cres. LN6: N Hyk 5G 21
Vulcan St. LN5: Wad 2G 27

W

WADDINGTON 3F 27
Waddingworth Gro. LN2: Lin 5G 11
Wainer Cl. LN6: Lin 2G 21
Wainwell M. LN2: Lin 2E 38 (2G 17)
(not continuous)
Wakefield Cl. LN4: Brace H 3H 23
Wake St. LN1: Lin 1E 16
Walbury Cl. LN5: Lin 5D 22
Walcot Cl. LN6: Lin 1K 21
Waldeck St. LN1: Lin 1A 38 (1E 16)
Waldo Rd. LN4: Brace H 2F 23
Walford Dr. LN6: Lin 1A 22
Walker Cl. NG24: N'wark T 1E 36
Walled Garden, The LN5: Harm 7E 26
Wallis Av. LN6: Lin 3B 22
Walmer St. LN2: Lin 3J 17
Walnut Cl. LN5: Wad 7C 22
Walnut Gth. LN3: Ree 5H 13
Walnut Pl. LN5: Lin 7C 38 (5F 17)
Walnut Tree M. *NG24: N'wark T 4E 34*
(off Winthorpe Rd.)
Waltham Cl. LN6: Lin 1G 21
NG24: Bald 5H 37
Waltham Rd. LN6: Lin 1F 21
Walton's La. NG23: N Mus 3B 32
Warburton St. NG24: N'wark T 6E 34
Warren Ct. LN2: Lin 7K 11
Warren La. LN6: With S 6A 26
Warwick Brewery NG24: N'wark T 5E 34
Warwick Cl. LN1: Sax 2D 8
Warwick Ct. NG24: Bald 4H 37
Warwick Rd. NG24: Bald 4H 37
Wasdale Cl. LN6: Lin 4G 15
Washdike La. LN5: Wad 7B 22
Washdyke La. LN2: Nett 2K 11
WASHINGBOROUGH 5E 18
Washingborough Rd. LN4: H'ton 6E 18
LN4: Lin 6G 17
Waterford Ct. LN3: C Will 1F 19
Waterford La. LN3: C Will 2E 18
Waterfront, The NG24: N'wark T 1C 36
Water Hill LN3: Fis 1K 19
Water La. LN1: Lin 5B 38 (3E 16)
LN5: Bass 2C 30
LN6: N Hyk 7K 21
NG24: N'wark T 6D 34
Waterloo La. LN6: Skel 4F 15
Waterloo St. LN6: Lin 5D 16
Watermill La. LN2: Nett 2B 12
Waters Edge NG24: N'wark T 5E 34
Waterside NG23: N Mus 4C 32
Waterside Nth. LN2: Lin 5C 38
(not continuous)
Waterside Shop. Cen. LN2: Lin 5C 38 (3F 17)
Waterside Sth. LN5: Lin 5C 38 (3F 17)
Waterwheel La. LN4: Bran 5D 24
Watery La. LN2: Dunh 3E 4
Watling Cl. LN4: Brace H 5G 23
Wavell Dr. LN3: Lin 2A 18
Wavell Rd. LN3: Lin 2K 17
Waverley Av. LN6: Lin 4K 21
Weaver Rd. LN6: Lin 2F 21
Weavers, The NG24: N'wark T 2A 36
Webb St. LN5: Lin 6D 16
Webster Cl. LN6: Lin 2A 22
Wedgewood Cl. LN6: Lin 7H 15
Wedgewood Gro. LN6: Lin 7H 15
Wedgewood Rd. LN6: Lin 7H 15
Wegberg Rd. LN4: Noct 5C 28
Weir Farm Paddock LN2: Scot 6H 5
Weir St. LN5: Lin 6D 16
Welbeck Av. NG24: N'wark T 6E 34
Welbeck St. LN2: Lin 3H 17
Welbourn Gdns. LN2: Lin 5G 11
Welland Cl. NG24: N'wark T 5F 35
Welland Rd. LN1: Lin 5D 10
Wellhead La. LN4: Noct 6A 28
WELLINGORE 6H 31
Wellingore Rd. LN2: Lin 5F 11
Wellington Cl. LN6: Skel 2E 14
Wellington Rd. NG24: N'wark T 7E 34
Wellington Sq. LN5: Wad 3G 27
Wellington St. LN1: Lin 2D 16
Well La. LN2: Lin 3C 38 (2F 17)
Wells, The LN2: Welt 2D 4
Wells Cl. LN4: Wash 5G 19
Wells Ct. LN1: Sax 3G 9
Wells Dr. LN4: Brace H 3H 23
Wellsykes La. LN4: Wash 7C 18
WELTON 2C 4
Welton Gdns. LN2: Lin 5F 11
Welton Manor Golf Course 1C 4
Welton Rd. LN2: Dunh, Nett 7A 4
Wentworth Cl. LN1: Sax 2D 8
LN4: H'ton 5G 19
Wentworth Cnr. NG24: N'wark T 3C 36
Wentworth Dr. LN2: Dunh 4E 4
Wentworth Way LN6: Lin 7F 15
Wesleyan Ct. LN2: Lin 4D 38 (3F 17)
Wesley Cl. LN4: Meth 4H 29
NG24: Bald 4H 37
Wesley Rd. LN3: C Will 7D 12
Westacre Ct. LN2: N Gre 5C 12
West Bank LN1: Sax 4C 8
West Bight LN1: Lin 1C 38 (1F 17)
Westbourne Gro. LN1: Lin 4A 38 (3D 16)
Westbrooke Cl. LN6: Lin 6B 16
Westbrooke Rd. LN6: Lin 6B 16
Westbrook La. NG23: Coll 6G 33
Westcliffe St. LN1: Lin 7D 10
Westcroft Dr. LN1: Sax 2E 8
West Dr. LN2: Scot 1G 13
Western Av. LN1: Sax 2D 8
LN4: Brace H 4G 23
LN6: Lin 6B 16
Western Cres. LN6: Lin 6B 16
Western La. LN6: Skel 1D 14
Westfield App. LN2: N Gre 5C 12
Westfield Av. LN2: N Gre 5D 12
Westfield Cl. LN4: Meth 4J 29
Westfield Dr. LN2: N Gre 5C 12
West Fld. La. LN6: T Hill 7B 20
Westfield La. LN3: C Will, Ree 5E 12
NG23: Coll 4F 33
Westfield St. LN1: Lin 3D 16
Westgate LN1: Lin 1B 38 (1E 16)
Westhall Cl. LN5: Carl M 6C 30
Westhall Rd. LN2: Welt 1C 4
Westholm LN3: C Will 1G 19
Westholm Cl. LN2: Lin 5K 11
West Mill Gate LN3: C Will 7G 13
Westminster Dr. LN4: Brace H 3H 23
Westminster Ho. *LN2: Lin 5G 11*
(off Welton Gdns.)
Westminster Rd. LN6: N Hyk 3H 21
West Pde. LN1: Lin 3A 38 (2D 16)
West St. LN5: Well 6H 31
West Vw. NG24: Bald 4H 37
Westway LN2: Nett 2C 12
Westwick Dr. LN6: Lin 7B 16
Westwick Gdns. LN6: Lin 1B 22
Westwood Cl. LN6: Lin 6A 16
Westwood Dr. LN6: Lin 6A 16
Wetherby Cres. LN6: Lin 3K 21
Wetsyke La. NG24: Bald 5J 37
Weymouth Cl. LN5: Lin 4D 22
Wharf, The NG24: N'wark T 6D 34
Wharf East LN5: Lin 3E 16
Wharfedale Dr. LN6: N Hyk 4K 21
Wheatfield Rd. LN6: Lin 5G 15
Wheatley La. LN5: Carl M 7B 30
NG23: Coll 7J 33
Wheatsheaf Av. NG24: N'wark T 3F 35
Wheelwright La. LN4: H'ton 7G 19
WHISBY 3A 20
Whisby Cross Roads LN6: Whi 3E 20
Whisby Crossroads LN6: Whi 2A 20
Whisby Nature Pk. 5C 20
Whisby Rd. LN6: Dodd, Whi 6A 14
LN6: Lin, Whi 3B 20
Whisby Way LN6: Lin 2G 21
Whisby Way Bus. Cen. LN6: Lin 2G 21
Whitebeam Dr. LN6: With S 7A 26
Whitefriars Bus. Cen. LN5: Lin 6B 38
Whitefriars Cl. LN2: Lin 7A 12
Whitefriars Rd. LN2: Lin 7A 12
Whitehall Cres. LN4: Brace H 3F 23
Whitehall Gro. LN1: Lin 3A 38 (2E 16)
Whitehall Ter. LN1: Lin 3A 38
(not continuous)
White Hart La. NG23: Coll 4G 33
White Hart Yd. *NG24: N'wark T 7D 34*
(off Market Pl.)
White La. LN5: Harm 7F 27
Whitemoor La. NG23: Coll 7G 33
Whites La. LN5: Bass 4C 30
Whitethorn Gro. LN6: Lin 5G 15
Whitfield St. NG24: N'wark T 1E 36
Whitley Cl. LN6: Skel 2E 14
Whittle Cl. NG24: N'wark T 5G 35
Whomsley Cl. NG24: N'wark T 7H 35
Wickenby Cl. LN6: N Hyk 4A 22
Wickenby Cres. LN1: Lin 6E 10
Wigford Way LN1: Lin 5B 38 (3E 16)
LN5: Lin 5B 38 (3E 16)
Wigsley Cl. LN6: Lin 1H 21
Wigsley Rd. LN6: Lin 1H 21
Wilford Cl. NG24: N'wark T 7F 35
Wilfred Av. NG24: New B 4G 37
William Bailey Ho. NG23: Coll 4H 33
William Hall Way NG24: Bald 7J 37
William Ho. LN6: Lin 3D 16
Williams La. NG24: Bald 6J 37
Williamson St. LN1: Lin 1F 17
William St. LN1: Sax 3E 8
NG24: N'wark T 1E 36
William St. Bus. Pk. LN1: Sax 3F 9
Willingham Av. LN2: Lin 5F 11

A-Z Lincoln 55

Willis Cl. LN1: Lin 1A 38 (1E 16)
Willis Rd. NG24: N'wark T 3D 36
Willis Ter. LN1: Lin 1A 38 (1E 16)
Willoughby La. LN5: Wad 6C 22
Willow Cl. LN1: Sax 3F 9
   LN6: Skel 3F 15
Willow Cotts. NG24: N'wark T 2A 36
Willow Ct. LN4: Brace H 4E 18
   LN4: Wash 4B 32
Willow Dr. NG23: N Mus 2C 12
Willowfield Av. LN2: Nett 1G 29
Willow La. LN4: Duns 3C 24
Willow Rd. LN4: Bran 5K 21
   LN6: N Hyk 3G 37
   NG24: New B
Willow Tree Cl. LN5: Lin 1D 22
Willowtree Gdns. LN6: Lin 6G 15
Willow Way LN2: Welt 2D 4
Wilson Ho. NG24: N'wark T 4D 36
Wilson St. LN1: Lin 1E 16
   NG24: N'wark T 6D 34
Winchester Cl. LN4: Brace H 3H 23
Winchester Ct. LN6: N Hyk 7H 21
Winchester Dr. LN4: Wash 5E 18
Winchilsea Av. NG24: N'wark T 1E 36
Windermere Av. LN6: N Hyk 5A 22
Windermere Rd. LN2: Lin 5J 11
Windmill Cl. LN5: Wad 4F 27
Windmill Vw. LN1: Lin 1A 38 (1E 16)
Windsor Av. NG24: N'wark T 2C 36
Windsor Cl. LN2: Scot 1H 13
   NG23: Coll 4H 33
Windsor Ho. LN2: Lin 6G 11
Windsor Pk. Cl. LN6: N Hyk 6K 21
Windsor Rd. NG24: N'wark T 1D 36
Wingrave St. LN1: Lin 7D 10
Winniffe Gdns. LN2: Lin 6K 11
Winnowsty La. LN2: Lin 2E 38 (2G 17)
Winn St. LN2: Lin 3G 17
Winstanley Dr. NG24: N'wark T 7J 35
Winster Cl. LN2: Lin 4G 11
Winston Ct. NG24: N'wark T 3C 36
Winterdale Cl. NG24: N'wark T 6H 35
Winterton Ho. LN6: Lin 7K 15
WINTHORPE 1H 35
Winthorpe Cl. LN6: Lin 7H 15
Winthorpe Gro. LN6: Lin 7H 15
Winthorpe Rd. LN6: Lin 7H 15
   NG24: N'wark T 4F 35
   (not continuous)
Winton Rd. LN5: Nav 5J 31
Wire Hill La. LN8: Wrag 2H 7

Wisdom Cl. NG24: Bald 6K 37
Wiseholme Rd. LN6: Skel 4F 15
Wisteria Av. LN4: Bran 1F 21
Witchford Cl. LN6: Lin 1F 21
Witchford Rd. LN6: Lin 2D 22
Witham Cl. LN6: Lin 5F 35
   NG24: N'wark T 5F 35
Witham Ct. LN5: Lin 5D 16
WITHAM COURT 6A 22
Witham M. LN5: Lin 7A 38 (4E 16)
Witham Pk. LN5: Lin 4H 17
Witham Park Ho. LN5: Lin 4G 17
Witham Point LN3: Lin 3A 18
Withams, The LN5: Lin 2D 22
WITHAM ST HUGHS 6A 26
Witham Vw. LN4: Wash 4C 18
Witham Wharf LN5: Lin 5B 38
Wittering Cl. LN6: Lin 1H 21
Woburn Av. LN1: Lin 7E 10
Wold Vw. LN2: Nett 1C 12
Wolfit Av. NG24: Bald 4J 37
Wolsey Rd. NG24: N'wark T 4E 34
Wolsey Way LN2: Lin 5J 11
Woodbank LN6: Skel 1E 14
Woodburn Cl. LN1: Lin 5E 10
Woodburn Pl. LN5: Lin 7A 38
Woodburn Vw. LN1: Lin 5E 10
Woodchester Ct. LN6: N Hyk 7F 21
Woodcock La. LN1: Burt W 6H 9
Woodcock Ter. NG24: Bald 6J 37
   (off Goldstraw La.)
Woodcroft LN6: S Hyk 7E 20
Woodcroft Rd. LN1: Sax 2D 8
Woodfield Av. LN6: Lin 6F 15
Woodfield Cl. LN6: Lin 5G 15
Woodhall Cres. LN1: Sax 2D 8
Woodhall Dr. LN2: Lin 5F 11
Woodhill Rd. NG23: Coll 3H 33
Woodland Av. LN6: Skel 4F 15
Woodland La. LN4: Noct 5C 28
Woodlands NG24: Wint 1H 35
Woodlands, The
   NG24: N'wark T 7J 35
Woodlands Cl. LN4: Pott 3A 28
   NG24: N'wark T 2C 36
Woodland Vw. LN2: Lin 2G 17
Wood La. LN6: S Hyk 6E 20
Woodpecker Cl. LN6: Skel 3E 14
Woodrush Rd. LN2: Lin 5J 11
Woods Ct. NG24: N'wark T 1E 36
Woods End LN2: Dunh 3E 4
Woodside LN4: Bran 3C 24

Woodstock Cl. NG24: N'wark T 7G 35
Woodstock St. LN1: Lin 2D 16
Wood St. NG24: N'wark T 7F 35
Woodvale Av. LN6: Lin 1G 21
Woodvale Cl. LN6: Lin 1G 21
Woodwards, The NG24: New B 2G 37
Woolley Rd. LN2: Scot 1H 13
Worcester Cl. LN4: Brace H 4G 23
   LN6: Lin 7H 15
Wordsworth Dr. NG24: Bald 3H 37
Wordsworth Rd. LN3: C Will 7D 12
   (off Newton Dr.)
Wordsworth St. LN1: Lin 3C 38 (2F 17)
Workshop M. LN5: Nav 5J 31
Worktown Ind. Units
   NG24: N'wark T 5F 35
Worthington Rd. NG24: Bald 5J 37
WRAGBY 3G 7
Wragby Rd. LN2: Lin 3E 38 (2G 17)
   LN2: Scot 2H 13
   LN3: New 4D 6
   LN8: Wrag 1F 7
Wragby Rd. E. LN2: N Gre, Ree 6B 12
   LN3: Ree 6B 12
Wrays Yd. LN4: Noct 6B 28
Wright St. NG24: N'wark T 7F 35
Wrightsway LN2: Lin 1K 17
Wroxham Cl. LN6: N Hyk 5A 22
Wyatt Ho. LN2: Lin 7H 11
Wyatt Rd. LN5: Lin 7D 16
Wyton Cl. LN6: Lin 1F 21
Wyville Wlk. LN6: Lin 7K 15

Y

Yale Cl. LN4: Wash 5F 19
Yarborough Cres. LN1: Lin 7E 10
Yarborough Leisure Cen. 6E 10
Yarborough Rd. LN1: Lin 2A 38 (1D 16)
Yarborough Ter. LN1: Lin 1A 38 (1E 16)
Yew Tree Way NG24: Codd 5K 37
YMCA Fitness Cen.
   Lincoln 5D 38
York Av. LN1: Lin 2D 16
York Cl. LN4: Wash 5F 19
Yorke Dr. NG24: N'wark T 5F 35
Yorke Lodge LN6: Lin 3D 14
   (within The Pavilions Student Village)
York Way LN4: Brace H 3G 23
Youngs Av. NG24: Bald 6J 37
Youngs Cl. NG24: Codd 5J 37

SAFETY CAMERA INFORMATION

PocketGPSWorld.com's CamerAlert is a self-contained speed and red light camera warning system for SatNavs and Android or Apple iOS smartphones/tablets. Visit www.cameralert.co.uk to download.

Safety camera locations are publicised by the Safer Roads Partnership which operates them in order to encourage drivers to comply with speed limits at these sites. It is the driver's absolute responsibility to be aware of and to adhere to speed limits at all times.

By showing this safety camera information it is the intention of Geographers' A-Z Map Company Ltd., to encourage safe driving and greater awareness of speed limits and vehicle speed. Data accurate at time of printing.